Classic Heathrow
PROPLINERS

T0386283

CLASSIC HEATHROW
PROPLINERS

TOM SINGFIELD

The
History
Press

Front cover: Two of the biggest airline operators at London Airport are featured in this colourful shot from 1962. Cunard Eagle's Britannia G-ARKA is towed past BEA's trusty Viscount G-AOYM. (Bob O'Brien collection)

Back cover: For any of you lucky enough to have spent time on the Heathrow roof gardens back in the 1960s and '70s, this image says it all. Here are families enjoying a day out for not much money watching the action at the UK's busiest airport alongside plane spotters, airport staff and thankfully some photographers to record such memories. It could also be quite smelly up there – standing in the open behind an airliner like this Vanguard starting up was unpleasant but certainly memorable! (Pete Cannon)

Frontispiece: Twenty Rolls-Royce Dart engines in one shot! Iraqi Airways had five Viscounts, with YI-ACL surviving until a wheels-up landing in 1973. (George Farinas collection)

First published 2023

The History Press
97 St George's Place, Cheltenham,
Gloucestershire, GL50 3QB
www.thehistorypress.co.uk

British Library Cataloguing in Publication Data.
A catalogue record for this book is available from the British Library.

ISBN 978 1 80399 099 6

Typesetting and origination by The History Press
Printed in Turkey by IMAK

MIX
Paper from
responsible sources
FSC
www.fsc.org FSC® C111584

CONTENTS

This book is dedicated to the memories of Peter Keating and Brian Stainer.
Without their superlative photographic efforts to record the aircraft at London Airport
in glorious colour, this book would be much the poorer.

ACKNOWLEDGEMENTS & THANKS

Once again I would like to pass my thanks to all those friends and contacts that have so kindly helped me source such a great selection of colour images. I have also pestered a smaller number of friends for help with the captions and text, a big thank you to all of you. Mike Axe, Adrian Balch, Gordon Bain, Fred Barnes, Peter Bish, Tony Breese, Paul Burge, John Cannon, Ken Dalton, Ron Daly, Peter Dance (Air-Britain), Trevor Davies, Tony Eastwood, George Farinas, Martin Fenner, Caroline Foden-Williams, Barry Friend, Steve Gensler, Peter-Michael Gerhardt, Dick Gilbert, Peter Guiver, Noam Hartoch, Malcolm Hemming, Peter Hillman, Steve Hill, Chris Huggett, Graham Hyslop, Stuart James, Chris Knott, Phil Lo Bao, Michael Magnusson, Ralf Manteufel, Peter Marson, Tony Merton Jones, Malcolm Nason, Dhamseth Pallawela, Jeff Peck, Pierre-Alain Petit, Ralph Pettersen, Dave Richardson, Eric Roscoe, Bob Ruffle, Paul Seymour, Rod Simpson, Daniel Tanner, Warren Vest, Richard Vandervord, Christian Volpati, Bob Wall, Dacre Watson, Dave Welch, Mickey West, John Whittle and Maurice Wickstead.

Special thanks must be made to my good friend Jacques Guillem in Paris, who so generously provided such a great selection of images. Sadly, Jacques passed away on 1 April 2023, leaving a huge gap in the aviation enthusiast's world. Thanks also go to Peter Marson for his unending support with caption research, Chris Knott and Paul Zogg for finding some great shots, Tim Spearman for sourcing some wonderful images and his impressive Photoshop skills and Tony Merton Jones for caption research and for his kind agreement to write the foreword.

FOREWORD

Every young lad remembers his first visit to London Airport. That magical moment as you first approach this great metropolis as a grand airliner of the day soars overhead, departing to some far-flung destination that you had only heard about in a geography lesson. As a 6-year-old travelling all the way from South Wales with my parents, my thrill was further enhanced by the wide array of vehicles, fuel bowsers, ground equipment and other colourful items that were needed to support the airliners of the day and their lucky passengers. Those smart BOAC-liveried Commer Avenger and Dorian coaches, the strange-shaped BEA AEC Regal buses and the many airline vans that scuttled around the airport were very different from the Western Welsh buses I was used to at home. But it was the airliners that really captured this youngster's imagination. As we stood on the roof gardens of the newly opened Queens Building in the glorious summer sunshine, the arrival of an Air France Viscount and the piercing note of its Rolls-Royce Dart turboprops has remained as a vivid memory ever since. We watched excitedly as other Viscounts, Bristol Britannias, DC-6s, Boeing Stratocruisers, Convair Metropolitans, Constellations and even a Dakota or two gave colour and drama to the aviation tapestry going on all around us. This was inspirational. Not a jet in sight, and spectators were positively encouraged to come and enjoy the wonderful spectacle offered by the world's greatest international airport. An informative commentary was delivered over the Tannoy system and tempting pull-out brochures were given away free by the fuel companies, portraying images of the many airliners using the services of Esso and Shell. That enthusiasm, kindled so strongly on that first visit, spawned a lifelong passion for following events at the airport and while the years have passed and the classic airliners of the 1950s have given way to a whole new breed of aircraft, that fascination remains.

It is, therefore, a great pleasure to write a few words to accompany Tom Singfield's wonderful panorama celebrating the golden age of air travel at London Airport. With his lifelong interest in the airport and encyclopaedic knowledge of all things aeronautical, no one is better qualified to compile this book. Such a busy airport means that the types and airlines that have graced the concrete at London Airport are many and varied and selection of the appropriate photographs must have been a challenging task, but within these pages there are many treasures for the discerning enthusiast.

Tony Merton Jones
Editor, *Propliner* magazine

INTRODUCTION

Welcome to *Classic Heathrow Propliners*, a book that celebrates in full colour many of the great propliners that have visited London Airport with an emphasis on the busy days in the 1960s and '70s, when so many airliners were propeller powered. In September 1966, London Airport was renamed Heathrow after the tiny hamlet of Heath Row that originally occupied the site, but, for many years, aircraft enthusiasts still affectionately called it LAP. That term has now disappeared to be replaced by 'The Row', which is matched by Gatwick's 'The Wick'.

It has been a real labour of love sourcing the very best colour images from contacts all over the world, but I am sure you will agree the result has been worthwhile. Like my previous books on Gatwick, I made a decision early on to only include colour shots, despite the availability of high-quality black and white images of types and airlines that were visitors long before colour film was common. Not every image is of the highest quality, but, back in the day, photographers didn't always have the best cameras and good-quality colour film was expensive, especially slide film. Most of the images herein are scanned from original 35mm colour slides, usually Kodachrome, a very much missed film of exceptional quality.

THE ONES THAT GOT AWAY

Some propliner types that visited London Airport deserve a mention here because no suitable colour image has been found to illustrate them. LAP's first 'service' was a British South American Airways (BSAA) Avro Lancastrian that departed on 1 January 1946 to Buenos Aires on a route-proving flight. The type flew the full commercial service ten weeks later. Sadly, no BSAA propliners have made it into this book.

◄ A sunny afternoon on the roof gardens with superb views of the airport action for families and enthusiasts alike. The hut on the right was where the commentator sat. (Author's collection)

LAP was privileged to receive a visit from the giant Bristol Brabazon on 15 June 1950. It stayed for two days and made a few demonstration flights. Despite the high hopes for the type to feature in London skies for many years, it was a disaster, both financially and aeronautically. Early propliner types operated by BOAC that were seen but are not illustrated included Consolidated Liberators (BOAC had six), HP Haltons (BOAC had twelve), HP Hermes (BOAC had twenty) and Avro Lancastrians (BOAC had twenty-one).

Another type from the 1950s that has failed to appear here is the Saab Scandia. Scandinavian Airlines System (SAS) did fly them to London a few times a week in the summers of 1953–55 before the Convair 440s took over. Only nine of the impressive SE.2010 Armagnac airliners were built, and black and white photos of a SAGETA Armagnac parked in the central area show that one visited in December 1956, but like the much later French-built Mercure, it was a financial flop. Extra capacity for Air France in the summer of 1955 came from another rare visitor, a Boeing Stratoliner from UAT (Union Aeromaritime de Transport). The Blackburn Universal (Beverley) G-AOEK was another type to only visit once in November 1955, returning from a Middle East oil-related cargo charter. An Egyptian civilian Siai-Marchetti SM.95 visited just once, as did an Ilyushin Il-12 from the Soviet Union. Other propliners not illustrated include the Miles Marathon, AAC1 (French-built Junkers Ju-52), Avro Lancaster, Avro Lincoln, HP Halifax and the Lisunov Li-2, which was a Soviet licence-built Dakota.

Many military and/or government-operated propliners from all over the world have visited, especially on VIP flights, but for space reasons they have been left out. Many RAF stations celebrated 'Battle of Britain' days with an 'At Home' event open to the public. LAP held several of them in the 1950s, and in September 1958 the appearance of an RAF Beverley and a Hastings were certainly rare visitors. One interesting military propliner movement was in 1964 when a USAF C-124 Globemaster brought in a replacement DC-8 lower fuselage section from the Douglas factory for the rebuild of the TCA DC-8 CF-TJM in BOAC's technical block. The DC-8 had run off the end of 28R and ended up in a cabbage patch!

SPECTATORS

Back in the late 1940s, the airport positively encouraged non-flying visitors to visit soon after the official opening on 25 March 1946. A public viewing enclosure situated beside the north-side control tower opened around 1947, possibly to deflect criticism that the new airport was an underused 'white elephant'. Very popular local scenic flights were flown from here in Island Air Services' Dragon Rapides between 1948 and 1956. The viewing area was a great success and it was moved to the central area after the tunnel opened. In addition to horse and pony rides (yes really), for the adventurous there was a tours section of the Ministry of Aviation that could organise private airport tours, although for half a crown you could join the fifty-minute coach tour from the enclosure. After 1956, spectators could climb the stairs up to the famous roof gardens above the Queens Building and the Europa building/Terminal Two.

FIFTY-YEAR CELEBRATIONS

Mention should be made of a very special day at Heathrow on 2 June 1996 when thirty-three aircraft made an impressive flypast to celebrate fifty years since the airport opened. The incredible planning for the flypast took several months, with a variety of aircraft chosen to represent some of the major types that had flown from the airport since its inception. All movements were halted while the cavalcade flew along the runway. The Battle of Britain Memorial Flight's Avro Lancaster was an appropriate stand-in for the Avro Lancastrian that made LAP's

first service, while other propliner types were first in the cavalcade with a DH Rapide, Bristol Freighter, DH Dove, DH Heron, DC-3, DC-4, DC-6, Viscount, Herald and HS748 before the jetliners followed, culminating in a Concorde alongside the Red Arrows and finishing with a Boeing 777.

CURRENT PROPLINERS

Propliners still appear at Heathrow to this day, but only just. Flybe went bust in January 2023 so its Dash 8s no longer appear. Norwegian airline Widerøe used Dash 8s occasionally until the beginning of the 2023 summer schedules when it moved to Stansted.

Although the glory days of the roof gardens are no more, there is still a spectators' area with parking at the Heathrow Academy building on Newall Road on the north side, just where so many great propliners parked up all those years ago.

Tom Singfield
Horsham
June 2023

◄ A 1950s' view of the north side parking area with the viewing area in the foreground. Visible are a BOAC Argonaut, Air India Constellation and Avro Yorks from Skyways and Hunting-Clan. Just visible on the left is the statue of Alcock and Brown, which is now at the Brooklands Museum. (Peter Marson)

1

TWO INTO ONE

One of the biggest shake-ups in British aviation history occurred in April 1974 when the two giants of the British airline world, British European Airways (BEA) and the British Overseas Airways Corporation (BOAC), were merged to form British Airways (BA) after recommendations by the Edwards Committee report. BOAC had provided excellent service for thirty-four years, while BEA had been around for twenty-eight years. Their legacy was huge and the aircraft they flew are remembered fondly.

▲   The huge fleet of nearly seventy Dakotas operated by BEA were given the class name 'Pionair'. Most aircraft were nominally delivered on 1 August 1946, the day BEA came into existence, and were used for services from Northolt. The first BEA Pionair service to operate from the primitive tents at LAP was in April 1950 but most continued using Northolt, with the last 'Pionair' service getting a good send-off in October 1954. The illustrated G-ALXN was given turboprop Dart engines in 1951 but was converted back to normal piston power in 1953. (AirTeamImages)

➤ Given the BEA class name 'Elizabethan', the Airspeed Ambassador flew its first commercial service on 3 September 1951 from London to Paris. The type's last BEA scheduled service was on 30 June 1958 when G-AMAF flew London Airport–Hannover–Cologne–London Airport. The twenty-strong BEA fleet amassed 31 million miles of flying and carried 2,430,000 passengers. Sadly, the Elizabethan is best remembered for the Munich air disaster in 1958 when twenty-three passengers, including many members of the Manchester United Football Club, died. Illustrated is G-AMAD 'Sir Francis Drake', which later flew for BKS Air Transport. It was destroyed at Heathrow on 3 July 1968 when it crashed into the terminal building, killing six crew members, including grooms and racehorses, while on a bloodstock charter. (Christian Volpati collection)

◀ BEA received its first series 700 'Discovery'-class Viscount in January 1953 and once the fleet had expanded, BEA started using them on its 'Silver Wing' first-class service from London to Paris, Nice, Malta, Lisbon and Gibraltar. This luxury service included the finest cuisine with complementary Moët et Chandon special cuvée champagne. The luxury Viscount services also included The Clansman to Glasgow and The Ulster Flyer to Belfast. Here is G-AMON in the original colours. (Stephen Wolf collection)

▲ The year 1953 was a significant one for the Viscount because BEA ordered a dozen of the larger sixty-six-seater V.802 aircraft. In total, BEA flew seventy-seven Viscounts of both the 700 and 800 series. BEA/BA's Viscounts were an incredible success story and play a significant part in the author's aviation history as it was in BEA Viscount G-AOHV (illustrated) that he took his first ever flight on 7 September 1970. (Author's collection)

➤ Even before its Viscounts had entered service, BEA had discussed proposals for a big brother type with Vickers. However, it took until 1956 for the deal to be signed for twenty Vanguards, consisting of six V.951s with 108 Tourist and eighteen first-class seats and fourteen V.953s with 135 seats in an all-Tourist layout. Illustrated is G-APEA when it was demonstrated to the press at LAP in the earlier BEA colour scheme on 7 May 1959. Advertised as BEA's first 'Airbus', Vanguard G-APEF operated the first commercial Vanguard service from London Airport to Le Bourget on 17 December 1960. (Adrian Balch collection)

◄ The public preferred jets and by the late '60s, the first conversion of a Vanguard to an all-cargo Merchantman had taken place. Eventually, nine V.953 Vanguards were converted either by Aviation Traders at Southend or by BEA using kits supplied by the same company. The first scheduled BEA Merchantman service was Heathrow–Stuttgart–Vienna–Heathrow on 7 February 1970. The last BA scheduled Merchantman service was made by G-APEJ on the night of 1–2 December 1979. (Martin Fenner collection)

▲ BEA operated nine different Argosy freighters, with the first three being delivered to LAP in late 1961, initially serving Milan on an ad hoc basis. Its hold was fitted with Rolamat floors, and with the use of specialised BEA ground vehicles it could be loaded directly from lorries through the fully opening nose or tail doors. BEA bought five Series 222s in 1964 to replace the earlier examples, which were sold to Hawker Siddeley. The last Argosy built was G-ATTC; it was bought in 1966 as a replacement for the crashed G-ASXL. Argosy operations stopped in 1970 when the type was replaced by the Merchantman. (John Coupland via Paul Seymour)

⋏   This shot of Canadair C-4 Argonaut G-ALHJ was taken in the fire training compound in July 1980. It eventually became too unsafe to use and was scrapped around 1982. It had been parked inside the BOAC maintenance area for many years and used for training engineering apprentices until replaced by a DH Comet. (Author's collection)

◄ Formed by order of the UK Government in 1939, BOAC managed to keep several of the long-haul Empire routes open throughout the Second World War. At war's end it had 170 aircraft of eighteen different types, so rationalisation was imperative. Government orders were to only buy British-built types despite BOAC wanting Constellations and DC-4s; so Lancasters, Lancastrians, Yorks, Haltons as well as various flying boats were the norm. BOAC received five L-049 Constellations in 1946 and later acquired the Aerlinte Eireann L-749 fleet. This is G-ANNT, a late production L-749 acquired from Lockheed in 1954, in a colourised image at LAP. (John Coupland via Steve Hill)

► The colourised image of Avro York G-AGSO 'Marston' is used in order that this significant BOAC type didn't get missed out in this book. G-AGSO joined BOAC in the summer of 1945 and was sold to Skyways in November 1957. The 1950s saw BOAC buying Handley Page Hermes and Canadair C-4 Argonauts. (John Coupland via Steve Hill)

▲ Available photos show that the first seven BOAC Boeing Stratocruisers were delivered in an all-over natural metal finish prior to painting up with a white tail fin scheme. BOAC's first scheduled Stratocruiser service from London to New York (via Prestwick) was on 6 December 1949. Fitted with sixty luxury seats and a twelve-seater downstairs cocktail bar, the Stratocruisers were a favourite with wealthy passengers. The final BOAC Stratocruiser colour scheme is seen here on G-ANTZ 'Cordelia', parked up in the BOAC maintenance area. (Zoggavia)

◄   BOAC's last scheduled service by a piston-engined aircraft was with one of its DC-7Cs in March 1961 but the type continued for another couple of years on passenger charters. BOAC could really keep up with the American-built airliners once its long-range Series 300 Britannias arrived. On 19 December 1957, Britannia 312 G-AOVC inaugurated a once-a-week first-class service from London to New York departing Fridays and returning on Mondays. On 31 March 1959, BOAC commenced a round-the-world Britannia scheduled service routing westabout via the Atlantic and Pacific. Britannia G-ANBI, seen in August 1962, flew the first scheduled Britannia service to Johannesburg from London Airport on 1 February 1957. (Martin Fenner collection)

➤   Viscount 701 G-AMOG is shown in full BOAC livery just after re-paint from Cambrian colours in April 1972. One of two leased from Cambrian in 1972–73 to connect Belfast and Edinburgh to Prestwick for international services, G-AMOG has survived into the twenty-first century and is currently dismantled in storage awaiting restoration at the National Museum of Flight at East Fortune, Scotland. (Angus Squire)

➤ Canadair CL-44 N228SW shows off its 'swing tail', which allowed loading of outsize cargoes directly into the fuselage rather than diagonally through a side cargo door. In 1963, BOAC agreed a complicated two-year lease deal for this single Seaboard World CL-44D-4 for use on transatlantic freight runs from London Airport to New York via Manchester and Prestwick. Seaboard trained around twenty BOAC pilots on the Forty-Four and they shared the flying with Seaboard crews. (Mike Hooks)

◄ About to touch down on 28R in 1978 is Viscount V.802 G-AOJF, looking pretty smart in its new BA colours despite being in regular service for nearly twenty-three years since its first flight in 1957. A couple of years later, it made its last flight to the BA maintenance base at Cardiff where it was later scrapped. (Peter J. Bish)

◄ The year 1974 was a momentous one for everyone at Heathrow as that was when the fiercely individualistic airlines BOAC and BEA were forcibly merged to create British Airways. Also included in the mix were the airlines in the British Air Services Group: Northeast Airlines and Cambrian Airways. Many of the 'new' fleet retained their old BEA or BOAC colours but with new 'British Airways' titles. BA had a huge fleet of propliners at the time of the merger, including nine Merchantmen, three Vanguards, thirty-two Viscounts and a pair of Skyvans that never came as far south as London. Here is Merchantman G-APEJ (top image) with 'British Airways Cargo' titles; and to show that not all airliners left Heathrow in one piece, here is Vanguard G-APEU (bottom image) being dismantled around the back of the BEA base in June 1975 after less than a year flying with BA titles. (Vernon Murphy, Fred Barnes)

2

BEHIND THE CURTAIN

In 2023 Britain, the sight of an airliner built by the Soviet Union is now pretty much confined to the occasional visit of a Ukrainian-registered Antonov An-12 or An-26 freighter at Birmingham International. Some airlines that were formally behind the Iron Curtain and appeared at London Airport have disappeared. Gone are JAT, Malév and TABSO, while ČSA died and was later resurrected. LOT and TAROM have managed to keep flying, while Aeroflot is currently banned from many countries.

◄ Built at the Moscow Khodynka factory, Ilyushin Il-14P CCCP-Л1729 (SSSR-L1729) was a surprise visitor to LAP on 24 July 1956. Fitted out as an eighteen-seater, it was operated by the International Air Transport Directorate in Moscow. Later flown by the Ulyanovsk Advanced Flying Training College, it was retired in 1972. (Adrian Balch collection)

▼ Arriving for work at the base of the control tower at Heathrow on an overcast 26 July 1970, the author was greeted by the sight of a grey Antonov An-12 flying low over the tower, in and out of the clouds. Approach control was in chaos with departures stopped and inbounds held off while two 'Aeroflot' (actually Soviet Air Force) An-12s tried to find the runway. Unable to land at Bristol Lulsgate due to the weather, they tried various diversions but ended up choosing Heathrow. With nobody on board with good English and no ILS equipment, they struggled to find the runway, causing an hour of chaos. A BEA employee who spoke Russian was found in Terminal 2 and he was rushed to the tower, where he translated ATC instructions to the crews and thus enabled them to land safely. The An-12s were due to collect the three Russian Yak-18s flown in the World Aerobatic championships at RAF Hullavington. The next day they were given clearance to fly to Lulsgate. The first one departed but the second was held on the ground because the first one was again causing chaos and ATC wisely decided to hold it until the first had landed! (Author's collection)

> Very few propliner types only made a single recorded visit. One that did was the Soviet Air Force's mighty Antonov An-22A CCCP-09319, which arrived from Moscow on 18 December 1988 to collect British-supplied aid following the horrific Armenian earthquake that occurred on 7 December, killing between 25,000 and 50,000 people. The An-22 was the largest propliner ever to land at London's airport. On the same day, jet-powered Antonov An-124 CCCP-82008 also arrived and the pair were parked on the north-eastern end of runway 23, one behind the other. Despite carrying Aeroflot titles, the airline never actually operated them as they all belonged to the Soviet Air Force. (Peter J. Bish)

◄ The first ever visit of a Tupolev Tu-114 airliner to the UK saw Tu-114D CCCP-76481 arrive at LAP on 8 February 1963. The aircraft, at the time the largest airliner in the world, was chartered by Roy Thompson to take 170 British businessmen to visit Moscow. Unable to reach the passenger doors using the highest available steps, BEA had to mount some steps on top of a baggage truck to do the job. On 7 October 1965, this example, CCCP-76470, brought in the Bolshoi Ballet company, and much to the amusement of hundreds of watching staff it burst a tyre on landing. The Tu-114 was the fastest propeller-driven airliner in the world, reaching speeds of 550mph (880kmh). (Author's collection)

◄ Having used its fleet of DC-3s for international passenger services for many years, JAT received its first forty-eight-seater Convair 340 in April 1954 and commenced a service to London on 17 June 1955 from Belgrade via Vienna and Frankfurt. The upgraded Convair 440 Metropolitan appeared on international services from 14 April 1957, and the airline's spring 1957 timetable shows a picture of Tower Bridge on the cover and a map with Convair 340s used for a service to London. However, the actual timetable fails to mention London at all! Here is DC-3 freighter YU-ABK in early October 1967 on a cargo charter. It was badly damaged in a forced landing on 8 January 1968 on a flight from Munich to Zagreb. (Author's collection)

▲ Established in 1928, the Polish national airline LOT (Polskie Linie Lotnicze) didn't manage to restart services to London after the Second World War until 1958, using Convairliners. SP-LPC, seen in 1961, was one of five Convair 240s. It was bought from SABENA in 1957 and stayed in service for ten years. Note the LOT emblem of a flying crane on the fin. (AJAviation)

➤ The summer of 1961 saw the appearance of this immaculate LOT VEB (Volkseigener Betrieb) Ilyushin IL-14 SP-LNH. Built in the East German Flugzeugwerke Dresden factory, it was delivered to LOT at Warsaw with two others in November 1957. One of twenty different IL-14s airframes flown by LOT, it was retired in 1972 and ownership was then transferred to the Soviet Union. (Jeff Peck)

▲ By December 1961, LOT was flying eighty-four-seater Ilyushin Il-18s on a twice-weekly schedule to London Airport via Berlin. Two years later the route was shared with its three Viscounts via Amsterdam or Berlin. This is V.804 Viscount SP-LVC. (Christian Volpati collection)

▲ The appearance of the Antonov 24 SP-LTH on a passenger flight on 31 March 1967 was probably to cover an unserviceable Il-18. Ten Il-18s were operated from 1961, with some still appearing at Heathrow in 1980. Five were converted to freighters, and the last few were retired or sold in 1991. (Jacques Guillem collection)

➤ In association with BEA, which flew Viscounts on the Budapest route, the Hungarian national airline Malév commenced services to London twice a week after it started to receive its new fleet of Ilyushin Il-18Vs in 1960. Malév operated eight of these long-serving 111-seater propliners, with four of them later converted to freighters. Seen here is Il-18V HA-MOH at LAP in August 1967. It crashed at night in fog at Budapest in January 1975 on a positioning flight from Berlin, killing all nine on board. Malév had commenced operations in 1946 but sadly it collapsed, owing $270 million in 2012. (Christian Volpati collection)

◄ TABSO Bulgarian Air Transport Ilyushin Il-18V LZ-BEL is seen waiting for the return trip to Sofia. The name TABSO relates to the earliest iteration of this airline that eventually became Balkan Bulgarian Airlines, which survived until 2002. TABSO was a joint Soviet–Bulgarian venture that started around 1949 with Soviet-supplied Lisunov Li-2s. The Russians quit the venture in 1954, and from 1956 the airline acquired Ilyushin Il-14s and from 1962, Il-18s. The Il-18s made irregular appearances at London on holiday charters or occasional VIP visits. A charter subsidiary called BULAIR started in 1968 to serve the Black Sea resorts of Varna and Burgas using Il-18s supplied by TABSO. The revised name Balkan Bulgarian Airlines appeared in 1968 with a new red colour scheme appearing initially on the new Tupolev Tu-134s. (John Coupland via Paul Seymour)

◄ The Czechoslovakian airline ČSA commenced services to London (Northolt) with DC-3s in April 1947, followed by Ilyushin Il-12Bs from September 1949. Timetable information reveals that scheduled ČSA Avia (Ilyushin) Il-14 services to LAP appeared around 1951 but these were not continuous until 1958, when their fleet of locally built Avia 14s appeared twice weekly. No Czech Il-14s were Soviet built; they were all built in Czechoslovakia under licence. This is Avia 14T freighter OK-LCA, which was retired in 1977 and sold in the Soviet Union. (John Coupland via Paul Seymour)

➤ ČSA switched to international jet services in 1957 after three Tupolev Tu-104As were delivered. At the same time, ČSA acquired twenty-five Avia-14s to replace its Lisunov Li-2s and Ilyushin Il-12Bs. Perhaps the most magnificent ČSA propliners to grace the Heathrow ramp were its Bristol Britannias. OK-MBB, seen here on 6 March 1967, was one of two leased from Cubana by ČSA during the 1960s and mostly used on the code-shared Cubana/ČSA services to Havana from Prague. (Jacques Guillem collection)

BENELUX BEAUTIES

3

The national airlines of Belgium, Netherlands and Luxembourg were all regulars at London Airport, operating a huge variety of propliner types. Most of them were medium-range types for European services but the tarmac at London Airport could also be covered in oil from long-range visitors such as Douglas DC-7s from SABENA and Super Constellations from Koninklijke Luchtvaart Maatschappij (KLM).

◄ After ten years of operations with BEA at LAP, Dakota G-AJDE was sold to Rotterdam-based charter company NV Scheepvaart en Steenkolen Maatschappij (SSM) in early 1961. Appropriately re-registered PH-SSM, it was repainted at LAP but the titles were quickly changed to Transaero Rotterdam. It was later sold to Martin's Air Charter and after suffering damage from a cargo acid leak it was broken up in 1967. (David Howell collection)

➤ Interocean Airways SA was launched as a subsidiary of the US airline Intercontinental US Inc in Luxembourg in 1960 to fly passenger and freight charters using C-54 (DC-4) Skymasters. Three seventy-seater Skymasters, including LX-IOA seen here on the north side, commenced operations in the summer of 1960, with this example first appearing at LAP on 26 July. It was back there on 16 September flying a service for Loftleidir after its DC-6 had gone sick. This C-54 had an interesting life, flying in the USA, Iran, Luxembourg, Norway, Germany and eventually Zaire. (Christian Volpati collection)

➤ This newly acquired Interocean C-54 LX-HEP carried ONUC titles during a visit in May 1961, two months after similarly marked LX-TEL had passed through en route to the Congo. ONUC stood for Opération des Nations Unies au Congo (United Nations Operation in the Congo), which operated between 1960 and 1964. ONUC was reportedly the largest, most complex, and most expensive UN peacekeeping mission during the Cold War. Altogether Interocean flew thirteen C-54s, two Carvairs, a DC-6, a DC-7 and a Constellation. (Author's collection)

◄ Dutch national airline KLM made its inaugural flight from London (Croydon) to Amsterdam in 1920 using a British-registered De Havilland DH.16 carrying two British journalists and a bundle of newspapers. London to Amsterdam is probably the longest-running commercial air route in the world. KLM commenced DC-3 operations in 1936 but during the Second World War many were destroyed by German bombing, although some escaped to the UK to restart services. This is PH-DAI in August 1962 on an early morning freight service from Amsterdam. (Christian Volpati collection)

◄ KLM didn't immediately switch to using LAP when it opened in 1946 but remained using Northolt and Croydon until 1948, when eight DC-4 flights a day were timetabled from Amsterdam. Awaiting passengers to Amsterdam in 1962 is Convair 440 PH-CGC, which had been delivered to KLM in 1954 as a Convair 340. After ending up in Venezuela in 1973, it survived in service until the mid-1990s. (Christian Volpati collection)

➤ This magnificent view of Lockheed L-1049C Super Constellation PH-LKX 'Nucleon' taxying along the north side taxiway was taken in August 1959. The aircraft was retired a couple of years later and eventually broken up at Schiphol in 1963. Note the logo on the forward fuselage showing KLM's fortieth anniversary badge and the main airline title 'The Flying Dutchman'. (J.J. Halley via Air-Britain Historians)

➤ The rare shot of DC-6B PH-DFK 'Jan Huyghen vans Linshoten' starting up on the north side was taken in July 1960, not long before it was leased to SAM Colombia. (Author's collection)

◄ This wonderful view from the roof of the Europa Building in the early 1960s shows DC-7C PH-DSD 'Black Sea' awaiting passengers bound for Amsterdam. Delivered to KLM on 18 May 1957, it was used on their worldwide passenger schedules to destinations as far as Santiago in Chile and Johannesburg. Although the Amsterdam to London route was mainly the preserve of Viscounts and, later, Electras, the DC-7C did appear on occasions as a replacement type. Note the lovely KLM Commer Cob 7cwt Series III van by the steps. (Author's collection)

◄ The turboprop era saw KLM serving LAP with Viscounts and from 1963 they were replaced with a rare type in Europe, the Lockheed Electra. This is L-188C Electra PH-LLG 'Neptunus', seen in 1967. This airframe later served in the USA, Sweden and in the UK with a variety of cargo operators. (Zoggavia)

▲ Luxair Luxembourg Airlines was incorporated in January 1948 as Luxembourg Airlines. The pilots and maintenance crew were British, with just the stewardesses recruited locally. It commenced operations with two twenty-four-seater DC-3s but services collapsed soon after and it wasn't until 1951 that Seaboard & Western's (S&W) DC-4s initiated services for the airline. The airline was reorganised in 1961 and it reappeared at LAP with its own DC-4 LX-SAF (illustrated) and a leased F.27 in April 1962. (Jacques Guillem collection)

▲ This Curtiss C-46 Commando was given the same registration at Luxair's original DC-3 LX-LAA. It was bought from Slick Airways in 1955 and leased to S&W for freight services in Europe. It was damaged beyond repair after its left undercarriage collapsed on landing during a training flight at Stuttgart-Echterdingen airport in June 1958. It caught fire but the crew managed to escape. (J.J. Halley via Air-Britain Historians)

◄ Luxair's sole Vickers Viscount 815 LX-LGC 'Prince Guillaume' was acquired in 1966 from Pakistan International and became a regular at Heathrow until it skidded off the snowy Findel runway inbound from Frankfurt on flight LG303 in December 1969, causing the nosewheel to collapse. Nobody was hurt but the aircraft was damaged beyond repair. (John Coupland via Paul Seymour)

▲ BOAC was cruelly known as 'Better On A Camel', TAP was 'Take Another Plane' and Belgium's national airline SABENA sadly came out as 'Such A Bloody Experience – Never Again'. SABENA's first service to London (Croydon) was in 1923, and by the summer of 1947 it was flying four daily services to LAP with DC-3s. The airport's first major accident was a SABENA DC-3, which crashed in thick fog at night with the loss of twenty lives in March 1948. The Dakotas were gradually replaced by Convairliners, here illustrated by Convair 440 OO-SCS having a break on the south side in February 1967. (Author's collection)

Another great shot from the Queens Building in August 1965 shows Martin's Air Charter DC-7C PH-DSO surrounded by a variety of ground vehicles, every one of them built in Britain. Fans of British-built commercial vehicles (I own a Morris Minor van!) will spot an Aer Lingus Hillman Husky and Bedford mobile steps alongside a Fortes Commer Walk-Thru and a Ford 400E Thames catering truck. PH-DSO was one of the last DC-7s built, rolling off the line in late 1958 for delivery to KLM. MAC changed its name to Martinair Holland in 1966 and from 2011 the airline became a cargo-only carrier. (Christian Volpati collection)

◄ By 1958, SABENA was flying scheduled DC-6s and Convairs from Brussels, with some routing via Antwerp. This is 'Super DC-6' OO-SDD in April 1960 having arrived as flight SN601 from Brussels. The former Belgian colony in the Congo saw several big Douglas propliners in operation with 'Air Congo', including this one. Later flying with the Congo/Zaire Air Force, it was scrapped at Ndjili around 1986. (Author's collection)

➤ SABENA's Fokker F.27-600 Friendship OO-SCA has a special place in the minds of many air traffic controllers who were at Heathrow back in the early 1970s. This aircraft operated a schedule from Antwerp and its crew were amazing at fitting in with all the fast jets. Any instruction given was followed without question and with great eagerness to please. This co-operation was often rewarded with an approach onto the southern runway, allowing the F.27 a shorter taxi to its stand in the Foxtrot cul-de-sac. When the service ended in 1972, the crew presented Heathrow ATC with a mounted R-R Dart turbine blade inscribed 'To London ATC with sympathy'! (Paul Huxford)

4

OTHER EUROPEANS

It is no surprise that most propliner visitors to London during the 'classic' days were from the close countries in Europe. As airlines from more distant parts of Europe started to arrive, Stan Little, the man in the commentary box on the Queens Building roof gardens, was kept busy learning how to pronounce some strange-sounding departure points and destinations. I wonder how he got on with Luqa (Looha) and Ljubljana (Loobeeaanuh)!

◄ In the early 1950s, Aer Lingus was flying its London scheduled Dakotas from Northolt but by 1956 the services had been switched to LAP. Here is DC-3 EI-AFC 'St Enda' with the lovely dark-green fuselage top around 1960–61. Note the Aer Lingus Friendship and Viscount behind. I wonder if there was an England vs Ireland Five Nations Championship rugby match at Twickenham? Prior to the last Aer Lingus DC-3 flight in 1964, they were used as freighters from both Shannon and Dublin to London. (Peter Marson collection)

➤ Aer Lingus had much larger freighters in the shape of three ATL-98 Carvairs, whose primary task was carrying vehicles and freight from Bristol and Liverpool to Dublin and Cork. This is EI-AMP 'St Albert' taxying at Heathrow on 23 August 1966. This aircraft later served with Eastern Provincial Airways in Canada as CF-EPX but sadly crashed in Labrador in September 1968, just months after entering service. (Angus Squire)

➤ Aerlinte Eireann (Irish Airlines) was an associate company of Aer Lingus formed solely to run transatlantic services from Dublin. Prior to starting, Aerlinte used a new L-749 Constellation for some Dublin–London services starting on 3 November 1947 but the Connies were rarely used and were soon sold. Move forward to 1957 and Aerlinte wet leased a fleet of five L-1049 Super Constellations from S&W. One of them was N1005C, seen here in September 1958. This aircraft is now displayed as a USAF C-121 at Dover AFB. (AirTeamImages)

➤ The first production model of the Fokker-built F.27 Friendship was delivered to Aer Lingus at Dublin in November 1958 as part of an order for seven Series 100 aircraft. They replaced the airline's Douglas DC-3s on short-haul services, mostly to the UK. Equipped with single-class seating for thirty-six (or forty when a bulkhead was moved), the Friendships were a great improvement over the noisy and ancient Dakotas. This is EI-AKC 'Fionnbharr', the other six F.27s remained in service until replaced by a fleet of used Viscounts in 1966. (Pete Cannon)

◄ The 1960 timetable shows the Aer Lingus Viscount flights from Dublin to London were operated in conjunction with BEA. Four times a week in the summer, the Viscounts set off from Dublin at 5 a.m. on what they referred to as the 'Dawnflight' so as to arrive at LAP at 6.25 a.m. These were followed by 'Dayflights', then from 10 p.m. by 'Starflights', which concluded with a weekend departure at 12.30 a.m., arriving at LAP at 1.55 a.m. At the height of that summer, the airline was flying a maximum of nineteen Viscount services to London from Dublin every day. This is V.803 EI-AOG 'St Finian', which joined the fleet in 1966. (Jacques Guillem collection)

➤ Dublin-based Aer Turas' lovely old Bristol 170 Freighter Mk.31E EI-APM was a visitor to Heathrow in February 1967, just four months before it crashed at Dublin killing both pilots. This was the aircraft's second spell of Irish operations, having been one of the five-strong fleet of Bristols used by Aer Lingus from 1952, when it was registered EI-AFT. This Freighter was most often used to carry racehorses. (Author's collection)

➤   Only three Douglas C-54/DC-4s were registered in Ireland, all of them operated at one time by Aer Turas. C-54B Skymaster EI-AOR was delivered to Dublin on 2 June 1965 to relaunch the airline's operations after the reorganisation of the company. Retaining its seventy-two-seat configuration, it found work throughout the summer of 1965 flying for several UK airlines including Cambrian Airways, which used it as a temporary replacement for Viscount G-AMOL following its crash at Liverpool. Aer Turas also operated the Britannia, CL-44, DC-3, DC-7, DC-8, Argosy and even a passenger-configured TriStar before it went bust in 2003. (Jacques Guillem collection)

◄   Established in early 1964, Shannon Air Ltd was an Irish airline backed by American money that flew both passengers and freight on charters. EI-AOC seen here was Shannon Air's second DC-7CF, leased in March 1965 from F.B. Ayer Universal Leasing Corp in Panama. That summer, it was based at Gatwick to cover the late deliveries of BUA's (British United Airways) new BAC 1-11s but its time with Shannon Air was short as it was returned to the lessors in December, the same month it was seen at LAP. (Christian Volpati collection)

◄   Air France was formed in 1933 and used the iconic Air Orient winged seahorse as its logo. Services from Paris to Croydon commenced that May, with prices for the one-and-a-half-hour flight advertised at six Guineas return. The January 1948 timetable shows DC-3s serving LAP but on the 19th Air France appeared inbound from Le Bourget with an SNCASE SE.161 Languedoc and by that summer LAP was getting four Languedoc flights a day from Paris. Fitted with thirty-three seats, it was not popular with passengers, and undercarriage and engine problems were very common, leading to its withdrawal from late 1949; but several examples soldiered on including F-BCUS, seen here, which retired around 1953. (Author's collection)

➤   A big step up for Air France came with the introduction of the DC-4 in 1946. The type was used for Air France's inaugural service from Paris to New York on 24 June 1946 routing via fuel stops in Shannon and Gander, taking twenty-three hours and forty-five minutes. The seven-times-a-day schedule to London from Orly boasted of an 'Epicurian' luxury food service. This is C-54B (DC-4) F-BHEH starting up in the central area in October 1958. (J.J. Halley via Air-Britain Historians)

➤ With French colonies spread across the globe, the airline needed long-range, reliable transports that were unavailable from French manufacturers, so in October 1945 Air France ordered four L-049G Constellations. Over the following years, the airline operated every type of Constellation, including the L-1649 Starliner. In total sixty-two Constellations/Starliners were used over twenty years of operations, finishing in 1967. Illustrated is L-1049G Super Constellation F-BHBI in 1966. (Christian Volpati collection)

◄ Established in 1968, TAT (Touraine Air Transport) became France's largest regional airline in the 1980s. It had merged with Rousseau Aviation in 1973 and in conjunction with Air France it started a six days a week Heathrow to Lille schedule. TAT's timetable for summer 1974 showed Heathrow services from Dinard, Nantes and Quimper all flown on behalf of Air France. Cleverly maintaining the abbreviation, TAT became Transport Aérien Transrégional in 1984 after yet another merger, this time with Air Alsace. Here is TAT Friendship F-BUFE in June 1973. (Author's collection)

▲ In March 1951, Air France ordered a dozen Viscount 700s and they became regulars at LAP. Years later, the Viscount was back in Air France colours when Cambrian Airways leased Viscount 701s G-AMOC and G-AMNZ to Air France in the spring of 1968 for operation on the airline's Lille to Heathrow route. (John Coupland via Paul Seymour)

▲ Looking magnificent in March 1967 is Air France Breguet 763 'Universal' F-BASV. This was one of twelve 763s ordered by Air France in 1951. Officially it was a Breguet 'Deux-Ponts' (French for two decks) but Air France gave it the type name 'Provence'. When set up for passengers, it carried fifty-nine tourist seats up top and forty-eight removable second-class seats on the lower deck, which could also be used for freighting. When Air France sold off six to the French Air Force, the remainder were converted to all cargo. Renamed the 'Universal', they were also used to carry Bristol Olympus engines from Bristol to France three times a week during the Concorde project.

The scheduled cargo service between Paris Orly and London that commenced in April 1965 was promoted by Air France, organising a different type of double-decker in the shape of a red London Transport RT bus complete with Air France adverts parking alongside F-BASQ for the benefit of the press. The type was withdrawn in 1971. A Heathrow controller recalls he asked a TWA jetliner to give way to a taxying Breguet, upon which TWA replied, 'Do you mean the fat cow?' To which Air France replied in a lovely French accent, 'It may look like a cow, but it flies like a bird.' (Brian Stainer)

◄ Rousseau commenced a Nantes–Dinard–London Gatwick route in 1970 and by 1973 this was switched to Heathrow. These services were flown on behalf of Air France with additional destinations Quimper and Rennes. Rival airline TAT started to take over Rousseau around 1973, with some HS748s and Nord 262s carrying dual titles, and by 1976 Rousseau had been totally absorbed by TAT. (Jeff Peck)

▲ Airnautic entered the air transport world in 1957 with a small fleet of an Airspeed Oxford and Consul before acquiring Vickers Vikings and commencing charters and IT services from Nice around 1958. Airnautic worked closely with Air France and Air Inter and was famous for operating the very last Douglas DC-2 in Europe as well as a fleet of five Boeing Stratoliners. Other types operated were DC-4 and DC-3. Money problems grounded the fleet in September 1965. Here, 1948-built Viking 1B F-BJES is parked alongside three Eagle Airways Vikings around 1960. (Brian Stainer via Peter Marson)

➤ Never a common type seen at Heathrow, Cie Air Transport's ATL-98 Carvair F-BOSU was a visitor in May 1968. Once flown as a DC-4 with Pan American, its conversion to a Carvair at Stansted was completed in 1966. Bought by Cie Air Transport from BUAF in 1967, F-BOSU 'President Malon' was test-flown at Southend on 6 May and delivered to Le Touquet the same day. It was later leased to Shell in Nigeria before retiring in 1970. It was broken up at Nimes in 1972. Note the logo on the forward fuselage that was, apart from the airline name, identical to Silver City Airways. (Brian Stainer)

▲ This 1957-vintage Viscount 806 G-AOYJ was leased to Cyprus Airways by BEA in October 1965 and repainted in Cyprus Airways colours. It was returned to BEA in May 1970 and flew in Cyprus colours with BEA 'red square' logos until sold to Cambrian Airways that October. In partnership with BEA, Cyprus initially flew to London via Athens using DC-3s from 1948. It leased a couple of Viscount 700s from BOAC Associated Companies in 1957 but the political situation in Cyprus was poor and the London route was taken over by BEA, with both aircraft returned without them entering service. The BEA Viscount service to Nicosia was the world's first regular one using turboprops. (Jacques Guillem collection)

◄ Iberia commenced a weekly DC-3 service from Madrid in May 1946, having flown a proving flight into Croydon on 23 April. The November 1947 timetable shows two direct flights a week from Madrid to London Airport in a DC-3, taking nearly five hours, plus five other flights a week from Madrid via Bordeaux. By early 1948, DC-4s had taken over the Madrid service and by 1950 they were also arriving via Barcelona or Paris. Anticipating transatlantic services, Iberia had bought three brand-new DC-4-1009s in the summer of 1946 for $400,000 each including EC-ACF seen here in September 1956. A long story, but in the 1990s, the author became the keeper of this aircraft's nose cone! It was donated to the 'Save the Skymaster' DC-4 Preservation Group at North Weald in 2000. (Jacques Guillem collection)

➤ Despite being called a Bristol Freighter, in Iberia service their four Mk.31 Freighters could be configured to carry forty-nine passengers or a couple of cars, or a combination of both. In an all-freight mode, it could carry 4 tonnes. This is EC-AHJ in the Central Area in early 1962. The Bristol Freighter is mentioned in the airline's history as carrying everything from Christian Dior fashion models to racehorses, live lobsters and aircraft fuselages! This aircraft was damaged beyond repair while flying for sister company Aviaco in a landing accident at Valencia in April 1962. (Mike Axe collection)

➤ The L-1049G Super Constellation EC-AQN appeared on 20 May 1965 when it brought in an engine for a broken-down Iberia Caravelle. Bought from KLM, it had been converted to a freighter in 1963. It was sold in 1967 and crashed in Biafra in 1968 during the Biafran War. (Zoggavia)

◄ After Fred Olsen took over the operations of Nordic Air in 1973, it gained a pair of Electras including LN-FOH, seen here departing Heathrow in May 1977. In 2006 it ended up with the famous Buffalo Airways at Yellowknife, and placed into service as C-GLBA. Fred Olsen flew six different Electras between 1973 and 1997, with Electra LN-FOI operating the final ever Fred Olsen flight on 29 December 1997. (Author)

▲ Note the total lack of aircraft behind in this evocative view of Convair 440 EC-AMV, complete with a full set of ground vehicles after arriving from Madrid in the mid-1960s. Note the forward airstairs and the First Officer by the tail completing the pre-flight visual check. The number seventy-five in a circle on the fin was its Iberia Fleet Number. (Christian Volpati collection)

▲ Now more famous for its cruises, the Norwegian company Fred Olsen Flyselskap A/S started flying in 1946 with three DC-3s and grew to include a Convair 340, Viscounts, Commandos, DC-6s and Electras. After failing to get approval to operate its new Viscounts on schedules, in 1957–58, it leased them to operators such as BEA, Austrian Airlines and SAS. Fred Olsen's hard-working fleet of three Curtiss C-46s, including LN-FOS seen here, had been retrieved from a wartime aircraft parking lot in Cairo and refurbished and uprated to C-46Rs in Venice before delivery to Fred Olsen in the winter of 1957–58. (Brian Stainer via AJAviation)

◄ Alitalia first appeared at LAP in 1953 when it arrived with Convair 340s once a week from Rome and three times a week from Milan. Its DC-7C I-DUVI was one of six in the fleet flown from 1957. In 1960, the DC-7Cs were transiting LAP en route to New York. Hidden behind the catering truck is a cheat line sticker showing the emblem of Rome advertising the summer Olympics of 1960. (Chris Knott collection)

➤ Starting in the spring of 1965, this scruffy Shannon Air DC-4 EI-ANL flew freight schedules for Alitalia linking Rome and Milan with London Airport every night. In November 1965, an engine failed and it diverted back to LAP on just three. After departure to Shannon for repairs, another engine died and it made an emergency landing back at LAP. It then sat waiting for two new engines, which Shannon Air could not afford. It was still there in February when the British Airports Authority seized it for non-payment of £15,000 in landing and parking fees. (Tony Breese)

➤ Loftleidir Icelandic was formed in March 1944 and initially operated only domestic routes. Its first flights to LAP were a series of four DC-4 charter flights in connection with the 1948 London Olympics. From May 1949, both Loftleidir and Iceland Airways (Flugfélag Íslands) flew DC-4s to Northolt, only switching to LAP in May 1957. The airline continued to operate this route until it merged with Icelandair in 1973 to form Flugleidir-Icelandair. Low fares were the airline's forte and many students were happy to cross the Atlantic via Iceland on what became known as 'The Hippie Airline'. Five Douglas DC-6Bs, including TF-LLE here, joined the fleet from 1959, replacing the DC-4s. (John Coupland via Paul Seymour)

◄ The magnificent Canadair CL-44D-4 started operations for Loftleidir in 1964; four of their fleet were later stretched to create the CL-44J, known as the 'Rolls-Royce 400 Jet Prop'. The only airline to use CL-44s for scheduled services, Loftleidir managed to squeeze 160 into the CL-44 and 189 on board the CL-44J. This is TF-LLH parked on the south side. (Brian Stainer)

Icelandair's first forty-six-seater DC-4 Skymaster TF-ISE arrived in 1948 and this was the first to appear at LAP in June 1953. In 1952, fierce competition between Icelandair and Loftleidir caused the government to divide domestic flights between them. An unhappy Loftleidir decided to cease all domestic services and concentrate on cheap transatlantic services. For the summer of 1957, Icelandair was flying a pair of V.759D Viscounts to London Airport direct from Reykjavík twice a week. Two Douglas DC-6Bs joined the fleet in 1961; this is TF-ISC in 1969. In 1973, Loftleidir Icelandic and Icelandair were forced to merge, leaving the name of Icelandair to survive. (Author's collection)

Austrian Airlines (AUA) leased four Viscount 700s from Fred Olsen in January 1968. These were used on a daily, direct Vienna–London service from 31 March. The leased Viscounts were returned to Fred Olsen in the spring of 1960 while AUA received its own fleet of V.837 Viscounts, including this one that was originally registered OE-LAM and named 'L.v. Beethoven'. OE-LAM was delivered to AUA at LAP on 3 August 1960, complete with a pair of 150-gallon 'slipper' tanks for extended-range operations. After it was leased to Austrian Air Transport (40 per cent owned by AUA) in 1964, it became OE-IAM (seen here) but retained full AUA colours. (Author's collection)

➤ Deutsche Lufthansa (DLH) commenced post-war airline operations on 1 April 1955 using a fleet of four newly delivered Convair 340s. On 16 May, one of them made the first post-war Lufthansa service to London, from and to Munich and Hamburg. This is CV340 D-ACOH in 1956. The two round exhaust pipes show this is a 340 – the 440s had rectangular exhausts. Five Convair 440s joined the fleet in 1957 and the four 340s were converted to 440s over the winter of 1957–58. (Tony Clarke collection)

⌃ If there is one classic propliner that merits its place in this book it is definitely this one! Douglas DC-6B OH-KDA was bought by Kar-Air in 1964 for passenger charter operations. In 1968, it was converted by SABENA to a swing-tail freighter and from 1 September 1970 it commenced a thrice-weekly night-time cargo schedule on behalf of Finnair that flew Helsinki–Heathrow–Manchester–Helsinki. In 1980, OH-KDA was struggling to get the right fuel at Heathrow, so had to depart Helsinki with a full twelve hours' worth of Avgas, allowing it to complete the return journey without refuelling. Its historic Heathrow status is because it made the last ever scheduled piston-engined movement at Heathrow on 27 September 1981 when it flew as AY033/034 to Manchester then Helsinki. Two days earlier it had performed a daytime flypast to say farewell and thanks to all the workers and the propliner enthusiasts who had enjoyed its visits. The aircraft amassed over 52,000 hours over twenty-four years of flying with Kar-Air. (Author's collection)

◄ Lufthansa's Convairliners were replaced by a fleet of eleven Vickers Viscounts from October 1958. The last to be delivered was V.814 D-ANAF in January 1962. An uncompleted sale to Nora Air Service in the early 1970s found the aircraft being used for Lufthansa technical training at Frankfurt Airport. It survived there until 2012 when it was transported to the incredible Technik Museum at Speyer where it is currently displayed on poles in exactly the same colours. (John Coupland via Paul Seymour)

➤ The queen of the DLH propliner fleet was the Lockheed Starliner. Introduced to its timetables from 1958, four examples were flown on luxury non-stop transatlantic passenger schedules but they only lasted until 1960 when two were converted to freighters and two, including D-ALER seen here, were sold to Deutsche Flugdienst. They were rare visitors to LAP, only appearing if the scheduled aircraft type was not available, or for extra capacity or as an extra flight at busy periods. (Chris Knott collection)

▲ Back in the 1960s, Lufthansa did not own any freighters, so in early 1964, it contracted US-based Capitol Airways to provide European freight services from a base at Frankfurt for six months. Capitol sent C-46s to service the new contract, which served London from both Düsseldorf (five times a week) and Frankfurt (six times a week), with the first aircraft arriving at London Airport on 22 March 1964. N9891Z was the only aircraft repainted in Lufthansa colours. The six-month contract was rolled out eventually to last five and a half years and used ten different C-46s. The amazing sound of twin Pratt & Whitney R-2800s could be enjoyed right up until 1969 when Lufthansa replaced the C-46s with its own Boeing 727QCs. (Brian Stainer via Christian Volpati)

◄ Continentale Deutsche Luftreederei was founded in December 1958 to operate passenger and freight charters from Hamburg to the Far East. Operations commenced with a pair of Douglas Skymasters (D-ABEB and D-ABEF) in 1959. Three more C-54s were acquired later but the airline was beset with financial problems, much of them brought about by some imaginative bookwork by the owners. Arriving at LAP on 26 August 1960, D-ABEF departed a couple of hours later as LL617 on a charter to Loftleidir of Iceland. (Tony Breese)

► Transportflug mbH & Co. KG commenced European all-cargo operations, many on behalf of Lufthansa, in the summer of 1965 using DC-4 D-ABAG. Based at Frankfurt, the airline grew so that by 1968 TF had four Skymasters, including this C-54B D-ADAR. After the German airline Allgemeine Lufttransport 'All-Air' went bust in October 1968, TF took over its three C-54s and later bought a pair of old Germanair Douglas DC-6As. Unfortunately for TF Cargo, Lufthansa switched to using its Boeing 737-200 'quick change' jetliners and TF stopped flying. (Tony Breese)

➤ Founded at the end of the Second World War, Transportes Aéreos Portugueses commenced initial operations with a pair of war-surplus DC-3s. TAP bought a fleet of four Skymasters in 1947–48 and in 1950 used them to inaugurate the Lisbon–London route. A major step up in the airline's fleet occurred in 1955 when it upgraded to Super Constellations, which replaced the DC-4s. The Super Connies continued to serve even after TAP received new Caravelles from 1962. They were finally phased out in 1967, making TAP the first European carrier to operate an all-jet fleet. (Zoggavia)

◄ One of the world's oldest and safest airlines, Finnair was founded on 1 November 1923 as AERO O/Y. The marketing name Finnair first appeared in 1953 at the same time as the airline bought forty-four-seat Convair 340/440 propliners. These were used from 1954 on a new route to London Airport from Helsinki via Copenhagen and Düsseldorf. Finnair flew ten different DC-3s, with OH-LCK lasting from 1955 until it was transferred to the Finnish Air Force in 1970. (Zoggavia)

◄ Four new Douglas DC-6Bs were purchased by Olympic Airways in 1958. They were initially flown on passenger schedules linking Athens with London, Orly, Frankfurt, Rome and Zürich. Comet 4Bs took over many of the schedules in 1960, but the DC-6s remained operational, with five second-hand aircraft being added in the mid-1960s. This is SX-DAI in 1963. In 1970, it was damaged beyond repair in a non-fatal heavy landing at Corfu that caused the nosewheel to collapse. (Author's collection)

➤ SAS was jointly owned by Denmark, Norway and Sweden. It made its first DC-6 service to London Airport from Stockholm-Bromma via Kastrup on 22 June 1948. The following year, SAS had enlarged its route network massively and London was then served by a daily DC-4 from Copenhagen, a daily DC-4 service from Stockholm via Gothenburg plus a summer DC-4 service from Oslo via Stavanger. This is DC-6B OY-KMI, seen not long before it was sold to REAL (Brazil) in early 1961. The words above the passenger door say, 'First over the pole – Around the world.' (Jacques Guillem collection)

▲ Iberia, in conjunction with BEA, flew a daily night-time mixed freight and newspaper service to Heathrow in the late 1960s and the '70s. Inbound from Madrid via Barcelona as IB2251, it was initially flown with a Spantax DC-4 and later a Trans Europa DC-4, although DC-6s and DC-7Cs were also used. DC-6B EC-BBK, seen here in 1969, was acquired in 1965 and converted by SABENA to swing-tail freighter configuration in 1968. (Author's collection)

Rarely seen in daylight, the Trans Europa Skymasters EC-BER, BCJ, BER and BDK operated the night-time Iberia 2250/1 freight runs and both them and the Spantax DC-4s were always fondly remembered as 'the Prince of Darkness' by the ATC tower staff thanks to their silhouette against the lights of the airport buildings and dim anti-collision and nav lights. One day when a Skymaster was taxying out in daylight for departure accompanied by the usual pall of smoke, a young ATCO in the tower wasn't used to seeing such sights and promptly hit the red button to alert the fire service. The captain then asked why was he surrounded by fire engines as nothing was wrong. Eventually he was allowed to trundle out to the holding point, where his run-up produced even more smoke. All quite normal and usually unseen in the darkness! (Robin Ridley collection)

Swissair was the first airline to use the fourteen-seater Douglas DC-2 in Europe, using it to connect Zürich, Basel and London (Northolt) from 1935. The 450-mile stage from Basel to London was the longest regular non-stop schedule in Europe. Post-war, the airline started buying DC-3 Dakotas (HB-IRX seen here was used as a freighter), which were regulars at LAP. (Jacques Guillem collection)

➤ Swissair's January 1959 fleet consisted of five DC-7Cs, seven DC-6Bs, eleven Convairliners, eight DC-3 and a single DC-6A freighter. DC-6B HB-IBU, seen here pulling on to stand in the central area in August 1962, carried between thirty-six and seventy-seven passengers depending on the seat arrangement. The star of the propliner fleet was the DC-7C 'Seven Seas', which extended the airline's routes to Argentina and Tokyo. (Jacques Guillem collection)

▲ Globe Air Lines was founded in 1957 and commenced charter operations from Basel with an Airspeed Ambassador in January 1961. With a small fleet of Ambassadors struggling with Berne's short runway, Globe Air bought a new Dart Herald in May 1963. This was soon followed by three more Heralds, including HB-AAH, seen here in the summer of 1966 having flown the night-time Lufthansa freight service, which was also flown by the Capitol C-46s. (John Coupland via Paul Seymour)

◄ In the early 1950s, Basel became a major airport for British charter carriers bringing IT groups to Switzerland. To compete with all these airlines, Balair bought a thirty-six-seater (2+2 layout) Vickers Viking in 1957 and commenced IT services on behalf of the country's major tour operators. In 1958, a second Viking HB-AAN (seen here at LAP on 11 September 1959) was acquired, allowing expansion as far as the Middle East and the Canary Islands. (J.J. Halley via Air-Britain Historians)

► Tellair (named after the legendary William Tell) was created in March 1968 in order to encourage international tourism to the Bernese Oberland in Switzerland. Tellair was able to start IT operations in March 1969 using a pair of Bristol Britannia 324s (G-ARKA and G-ARKB leased from Caledonian) and a Convair 440. Sadly, the enterprise was short lived as the Swiss authorities demanded that Tellair own its own aircraft; but with no investors found, the airline stopped flying in October 1969. (Martin Fenner collection)

5

FROM ACROSS THE POND

The classic propliners from the USA and Canada that appeared at London Airport prior to the appearance of long-range Britannias and Douglas DC-7Cs, which could traverse the Atlantic non-stop, all had to stop en route to refuel, particularly so when flying westbound against the prevailing wind. Gander in Newfoundland, Søndre Strømfjord in Greenland, Reykjavík in Iceland, Prestwick in Scotland and Shannon in Ireland all became vital transit stops for the early transatlantic airliners such as the Stratocruiser, Constellation, DC-4 and DC-6.

◄ Pan American World Airways first appeared at LAP on the official opening day, 31 May 1946, in a Lockheed Constellation. All previous Pan Am flights to London actually arrived at Bournemouth Hurn airport, nearly 100 miles from London! In 1949, Pan American introduced the world to the Boeing 377 Stratocruiser. This double-deck piston airliner offered sleeper seats and berths as well as a lower-level lounge. The Stratocruiser N1034V 'Clipper Westward Ho', seen here in 1957, was the height of 1950s flying luxury and would reign as 'queen of the skies' until 1958 when Boeing 707 jet service was inaugurated. (J.J. Halley via Air-Britain Historians)

➤ In September 1950, Pan American ordered forty-five DC-6Bs; this is N6110C 'Clipper Rival', still looking immaculate on a ferry flight through Heathrow in January 1967, one year before retirement. It stayed in the USA flying in Alaska for three years from 1973 before ending her flying days in Florida in 1979. (Jacques Guillem collection)

➤ In 1957, C-54G CF-IQM was operating for Wheeler Airlines on the major 'Air Bridge to Canada' series of flights from Vienna and London carrying emigrants and Hungarian refugees. Wheeler sub-leased CF-IQM to Nordair in 1960 and it flew many summertime transatlantic passenger charters until 1964, when it was converted to an ice reconnaissance aircraft. It was eventually retired in 1972 with over 35,000 hours on the airframe. (Author's collection)

◄ Built in 1969, this L-100-20 Hercules C-FPWR was delivered brand new to Pacific Western Airlines (PWA) and remained in service until it went to Cargolux in 1980 under a Libyan registration. PWA flew six Hercules into more than 108 countries and their last flight was in April 1984. The airline was founded in 1946 and lasted forty-one years until it was merged with Canadian Pacific and Nordair to form Canadian Airlines International. (Jacques Guillem collection)

◀ Originally a visitor to LAP when it was operated by KLM as PH-TDG in the late 1940s, this Lockheed L-749A became G-ANUZ with BOAC in 1955 and was put into storage in 1958. It was bought by the Babb Company in the USA as N9812F and in June 1960 it was leased to Miami Airlines as 'Mary H' and sub-leased to Loftleidir, which used it for its scheduled passenger service between Iceland and London between 29 July and 6 August 1960. (J.J. Halley via Air-Britain Historians)

➤ Trans-Canada Air Lines' Viscounts became the first ever turboprop airliners and the first British-built airliners to operate in North America. TCA (later Air Canada) flew fifty-one Viscounts, which all stopped flying in 1974 after two decades of impeccable and much-loved service. Air Canada V.724 Viscount CF-TGS was undergoing modifications and wing spar replacement in the Fields hangar between May and June 1969 as the Air Canada maintenance facility at Winnipeg was too busy to do the work required. (Author's collection)

> The visit of this smart DC-3A CF-CSC 'Arctic 7' to Heathrow in June 1971 was supposed to be part of a round-the-world tour by seven Canadian film makers who had been given a $375,000 budget by Canadian TV and a Hollywood film company to record a series of six travel documentaries in South America, Europe, the Middle East, Africa and Australia. The Flight of the Arctic 7 was to show the more adventurous side of tourism, including sand skiing in Chile and talking to head hunters in Colombia. It is thought that the Dakota never went further east than Europe before returning to Canada in November 1972, where it was destroyed by fire in 1975. (Peter J. Bish)

◄ Colourful DC-4 N30048 of Transocean Air Lines is seen under tow on the inner taxiway past Heathrow's oldest terminal, which was opened in 1955. The terminal had several names: originally called 'the South East Passenger Building', in 1956 an extension was given the name 'Building 2 Britannic'. Then the whole lot became 'No.1 Building Europa', which in 1957 became Terminal 2. A Transocean DC-4 inaugurated a scheduled cargo service from New York to London Airport on 1 March 1955 on behalf of Airwork Atlantic. (Chris Knott collection)

▲ Transocean Air Lines' (TALOA) Boeing Stratocruiser N404Q was parked in the BOAC maintenance area in June 1959 after arriving on a charter flight. This was the only visit of a TALOA Stratocruiser but this aircraft had once been a regular as BOAC's G-AKGL from 1950. Formed in 1946, TALOA became the largest non-scheduled US airline. It bought fourteen ex-BOAC Stratocruisers and converted nine of them to high-density configuration, with sixty seats forward and twenty-six 'sleeperette' seats in the rear. (Robin Ridley collection)

By the look of the amount of maintenance steps surrounding European Asiatic's Skymaster N9702F, it must have needed a lot of work by Field's engineers after arriving for a three-day stay on 3 August 1960. Bought in June 1960 and quickly leased out to another dubious operator, California Overseas Airways, from 17 July it commenced charters bringing American students across the North Atlantic from New York. However, it was soon seized by the FAA for carrying passengers without the correct paperwork. (Tony Breese collection)

Tucked away on a corner of the Fields apron on 20 May 1961 was Intercontinental DC-4 N30042. It visited many European airports operating ad hoc holiday charter flights from the summer of 1960 and was transferred to associate company Luxembourg-based Interocean Airways in April 1962 as LX-IOF. It was bought by Aviation Traders Ltd, who converted it into a Carvair at Stansted in 1969. This later flew for BAF, SF Air, Aero Union and Academy Airlines who were still flying it in the late 1980s. (Angus Squire)

◄ A very rare airliner to appear at LAP was the Martin 404 Martinliner. Displaying a small 'efm' logo on the forward fuselage, sixteen-seater executive version N636 owned by the E.F. McDonald Company of Ohio visited on 5 August 1960 and stayed for a couple of days. This was the first visit by a Martinliner to London. Built in 1952, it became N636X in 1965 and in 1998 it was painted in 'Pacific Air Lines' colours and based at Camarillo in California, where the author managed to get a ride in it thanks to its friendly owner/ pilot Jeff Whitesell. On 29 February 2008, Jeff made the last ever Martinliner flight when he delivered it to the Planes of Fame Air Museum in Arizona. (Angus Squire collection)

▲ Sadly there are no more airworthy Bristol Freighters, with the last ever flight when one was delivered to a museum at Wetaskiwin in Canada in late 2004. When Heathrow celebrated its fiftieth birthday in 1996, the illustrated C-FDFC took part in an incredible flypast on 2 June that will never be repeated. Months of planning saw twenty-four airliners plus the nine Red Arrow Hawks pass overhead runway 27R. Aircraft types ranged from a pair of DH Doves to a Boeing 747 and a Concorde. C-FDFC, seen here taxiing out to fly to Stansted prior to the flypast, was sadly destroyed in a take-off accident at Enstone a few weeks later. (Adrian Balch)

➤ Trans Canada Air lines' L-1049E Super Constellation CF-TGA makes an impressive sight as it taxies away from the north side sometime in 1958. First entering the fleet in 1954, TCA flew fourteen Super Connies of four different sub types – L-1049C, E, G and H. On 31 December 1960, the very last transatlantic TCA Super Connie flight flew Zürich–Paris–London–Montréal–Toronto, arriving in Canada on 1 January. A genuine TCA Super Connie is preserved at the Museum of Flight at Boeing Field in Seattle. (Zoggavia)

▲ The National Aeronautics and Space Administration (NASA) is a civilian agency of the US federal government responsible for the civil space programme, aeronautics and space research. Since its formation in 1958, NASA has operated over 150 different aircraft types – everything from a fixed-wing paraglider up to the mighty Boeing 747, which many UK enthusiasts saw with the Space Shuttle fixed to its roof at Stansted in 1983. NASA has active aircraft spread over seven airbases in California, Virginia, Florida, Ohio and Texas. Prior to 1969, NASA aircraft often only carried an unofficial identity consisting of 'NASA' followed by numbers that showed which base they were from. This Skymaster, NASA 427, was based at Wallops Island in Virginia when seen in July 1968 and was used to calibrate satellite tracking stations. (Angus Squire)

◀ Transcontinental and Western Air (TWA) first appeared in Europe in December 1945, when it flew a Constellation to Paris. The airline became Trans World Airlines in May 1950 and first appeared at LAP on 1 October 1950 using L-749 Constellation N6001C inbound from Idlewild. The Constellation's big brother L-1649 Starliner – here is N7305C in 1958 – was able to fly non-stop in both directions across the Atlantic. TWA Starliners were regular arrivals at LAP, with some appearing after a non-stop 'over the pole' flight from Los Angeles and San Francisco. On 1 October 1957, Starliner N7307C departed LAP and set a new world record for the longest ever non-stop scheduled commercial flight to San Francisco, taking twenty-three hours and twenty-one minutes. (Zoggavia)

➤ Seen here in December 1965, TWA's unique Paris-based Fairchild C-82 Packet N9701F 'Ontos' ('The Thing' in Greek) was used for sixteen years from 1956 as a flying repair station and to carry spare engines for the TWA fleet. Much modified in Paris in 1956 with a dorsal jet engine, more powerful engines and a host of other mods, it was a regular and very welcome sight in London. (Author's collection)

➤ The 1969-vintage Lockheed L-100 Series 20 Hercules N7984S of Southern Air Transport was seen in September 1970 next to its cargo of a jet engine. Based in Miami, SAT carried out hundreds of life-saving relief flights all over the world but were probably most famous for being used by the CIA in the Iran-Contra affair in the mid-1980s. SAT flew a total of twenty-three L-100 Hercules before going bankrupt in 1998 and later its assets were bought by Southern Air. (Paul Huxford)

◄ The visit of American Airlines DC-6 N90703 in full colours in October 1960 was a rare spot as American didn't get permission to operate services to London until 1982. Bought from American by Field Aircraft Services, this very early example was first flown in 1946 and was intended for sale to Trans Arabian Airways as G-ARFU. That never happened and a couple of months later it was sold to Air Jordan as JY-ACF. The author managed to catch up with this machine during a visit to the fire school at Hal Far in Malta in January 1983, where it was eventually burnt in the late 1990s. (Angus Squire)

International Airlines Inc. was a mysterious US charter airline that the worldwide web seems to have ignored. Founded in California in 1961, internal charters commenced that September with a DC-6. A base at Templehof saw them flying German tourists to European holiday destinations with a pair of DC-6s, and they also operated a freighter DC-4. DC-6A N1281, seen here outside Fields with No.1 engine missing on 5 April 1964, had arrived as 'IL281' two days earlier and didn't leave until the 11th. After a year operating a DC-7C and DC-7CF, the company disappeared in late 1966. (Author's collection)

Formed as Riddle Airlines in 1945, cargo charter operator Airlift International acquired Slick Airways in 1968. Based in Miami, Airlift bought the first of four Hercules in 1967. This is brand-new L-100/L-382E Hercules N9254R on 16 July 1967. That year, when one arrived at San Juan PR from New York, the Airlift team there created an unofficial world record for 'turning round' a cargo plane when they unloaded and loaded 44,000lb of freight in nine minutes! The airline entered Chapter 11 bankruptcy in 1981, then reappeared with Friendships and DC-8s before folding completely in 1991. N9254R ended its days with Angola Air Charter and was destroyed by a surface-to-air missile in 1990. (Daniel Tanner)

➤ Originally built as a T-29C Convairliner for the USAF in 1953, by the time the author shot ET-29C N93 in March 1977; it had already carried three other American registrations – N28, N247 and N248 – while operating for the Federal Aviation Administration (FAA). The FAA had about six Convairliners based in Frankfurt, from where they were used to fly checks on navigational aids such as ILS and TACAN at airfields in Europe and North Africa that were used by the US military. It was retired in April 1977 and returned to the USAF. (Author)

◄ Here is Maritime Central Airways (MCA) Douglas DC-4 CF-MCI during a visit in the late 1950s. This aircraft was the first former US military C-54 Skymaster to be converted to DC-4 configuration for Pan American and was delivered in November 1945. In 1953, MCA was Canada's third largest airline; it bought CF-MCI in April 1957 and flew it on the Hungarian emigrant flights from London to Canada. MCA had five DC-4s; one of them was destroyed in a tragic crash having departed London Airport for Toronto on 10 August 1957. It refuelled at Reykjavík and was en route to Montreal when it encountered severe weather and crashed, killing all seventy-nine on board. (Tony Breese)

◄ A regular visitor between December 1956 and April 1958 was Overseas National Airways C-54D N50NA. Mainly seen during the Canadian Air Bridge in the summer of 1957, it usually stayed overnight on the south side. ONA operated three different C-54s into LAP in this period and these were replaced by four new DC-6A/Cs. All the ONA C-54s and DC-6s had registrations ending in 0 (zero) N A so that they looked like the airline's initials 'ONA'. (Jacques Guillem collection)

▲ The largest overseas operator of the Bristol Britannia was Vancouver-based Canadian Pacific Airlines. Starting in 1958, it used eight long-range Britannia Series 300s to serve its trans-Pacific and transatlantic schedules. The first visit to London by one was on a special record-breaking non-stop flight from Vancouver by CF-CZA on 23–24 February 1958, taking thirteen hours and fifty-seven minutes. Here is CF-CZC 'Empress of Tokyo' during a series of charter flights to London in the summer of 1961. 'Empress' was also the airline's radio call sign. CF-CZC was sold in 1965 to Transglobe as G-ATLE. It was eventually dragged onto the grass behind the control tower at Gatwick and used by the fire service until it was broken up in the 1980s. (Author's collection)

➤ Seaboard & Western (from 1961 Seaboard World Airlines) was a regular sight at LAP starting right back in the late 1940s with transatlantic freight charters to Europe, which from April 1956 became scheduled freight services. Seen on 29 May 1960 was S&W's only DC-3 (originally a US Navy R4D) N91221, which was leased to operate freight feeder services from Frankfurt to connect with the transatlantic DC-4 and Super Constellation flights from May 1959 until late 1960. (Jacques Guillem collection)

▲ S&W's transatlantic freight service linking New York with Shannon, London, Amsterdam, Brussels, Düsseldorf, Frankfurt and Cologne was flown mainly by Super Constellations. A fleet of Skymasters and a lone Commando operated feeder services to the main European hubs from Prestwick, Paris, Zürich, Geneva and Hamburg. This is L-1049H Super Constellation N1006C, seen in 1960; one of eleven Super Connies flown by the airline. It was leased by S&W to several airlines until sold in 1965. (Zoggavia)

◄ The longest-serving of all propliners in the fleet was Curtiss C-46A Commando N10427, which flew from August 1956 until December 1970. By the time it was seen here in August 1965, the airline had become Seaboard World Airlines. (Author's collection)

▲ S&W's replacement for the L-1049H Super Constellation was the equally elegant Canadair CL-44D 'Swingtail' (N123SW seen here) around 1961, which in turn gave way to a fleet of DC-8 jet freighters from late 1964 onwards. Because the CL-44Ds could swing the tail open, they could carry items up to 85ft long. (Jacques Guillem collection)

➤ This much modified Second World War Douglas B-25 Mitchell N1042B 'Lively Lady' appeared in 1972. Fitted out as an airborne camera ship, it was used in a variety of famous movies including *It's a Mad, Mad, Mad, Mad World*, *Fate is the Hunter*, *Flight of the Phoenix* and *Catch 22*. Set up by Frank Tallman and Paul Mantz, Tallmantz Aviation Inc. bought 475 surplus military aircraft for $55,000 ($115 per aircraft!) in 1946 and modified a B-25 as a camera ship. N1042B was its second B-25 and it was crewed by a captain, a co-pilot, a navigator, a flight engineer, a director of photography and two assistant cameramen. Tallmantz Aviation was sold in 1986 and N1042B went to Aces High at North Weald in the UK. It was the primary camera ship used to film *Memphis Belle* in 1988–89. (Author's collection)

▲ Wheeler Airlines was founded in 1921 in Quebec to support fishermen and hunters using bush planes. The airline was considered to be Canada's first airline and grew to become the second largest aviation company in Canada, with four separate divisions covering bush operations, helicopters, agriculture and transport. A contract to support the massive DEW Line project saw it buy its first C-54 in 1955. Passenger charters, including a massive series of flights full of British people emigrating to Canada and Hungarians fleeing their country's uprising, followed in 1957. C-54A Skymaster CF-WAL, seen here, was bought in March 1957 to support the flights. (Author's collection)

◄   Founded as All American Airways in 1948, US supplemental carrier Saturn Airways bought this new Lockheed L-100-30 (L-382G) 'Super Hercules' N15ST in 1971 and gave it the name 'Barney G'. One of sixteen Hercules flown by Saturn, N15ST is seen here on a freight charter in May 1972. N15ST later flew with Trans International, Transamerica and Southern Air Transport, which sadly lost it in a take-off crash at Kelley Air Force Base Texas in 1986 killing all three on board. (Author's collection)

➤   Founded by 'Jack' Conroy, Aero Spacelines Inc. was a US aircraft manufacturer forever associated with the Guppy outsize freighters that it converted from Boeing Stratocruisers. Specifically built for NASA to transport space exploration vehicles, the first conversion was the one-off Pregnant Guppy N1024V in 1962. This is Pratt & Whitney piston-powered Mini Guppy N1037V, which was parked up for six days in November 1969. This aircraft has survived and is now on display in Oregon. (Angus Squire)

6

A LONG WAY FROM HOME

Being the major international airport for the whole of the UK, London Airport was a prime destination for many international airlines from all over the world. In addition to passenger services, London was a major hub for freight airliners but with the use of belly holds in wide-bodied jets, the cargo airlines have virtually disappeared from the Heathrow cargo area. London Airport was also an occasional transit stop for delivery flights, mostly from the USA to Europe, as well as a Customs clearance airport for airliners sold from the UK to foreign airlines.

◄ Qantas L-749 Constellation VH-EAD was the first to fly the schedule all the way to London from Sydney on 1 December 1947. The three-times-a-fortnight service required seven stops en route – Darwin, Singapore, Calcutta, Karachi, Cairo, Castel Benito (Tripoli) and Rome – with a flight time of fifty-eight hours over more than four days. The aircraft carried twenty-nine passengers, three pilots, one navigator, two flight engineers and three cabin crew. Super Constellations replaced the L-749s on the London route from August 1954. On 17 January 1958, Qantas commenced its first scheduled round-the-world flight from London to London using a pair of L-1049G Super Constellations, VH-EAO and EAP. The illustrated L-1049H VH-EAM (plus VH-EAN) were initially used on tourist-class services, but were transferred to the weekly all-cargo service in conjunction with BOAC in 1959–60. (J.J. Halley via Air-Britain Historians)

➤ A rare sight at LAP was a Qantas Skymaster. The illustrated VH-EDA parked in the BOAC hangar in August 1964 was on a cargo flight from Sydney via Rome and returned home three days later. Many years earlier, Qantas DC-4s VH-EBK and EBL had visited shortly after they had been delivered in April–May 1949. They were chartered by BOAC to fly some Sydney–London services as insufficient BOAC Constellations were available. (Author's collection)

Somali Airlines was established in March 1964 by the country's government in equal share with Alitalia. Initially operating Dakotas and Cessnas, in 1968 Alitalia provided a pair of Viscount 785s, which were then registered 6OS-AAJ and 6OS-AAK. This is 6OS-AAK on 21 May 1969 awaiting delivery to Mogadishu, having arrived from Rome for servicing by Huntings. 6OS-AAK ended its days on the dump at Mogadishu after it was retired in 1977. (Fred Barnes)

It looks like some serious maintenance to the number one engine of Super Constellation AP-AFS of Pakistan International Airlines in 1960. PIA received three new L-1049C Super Connies in early 1954 and they commenced a London service via Cairo and Rome starting in February 1955. In 1956, PIA was flying the weekly scheduled PK505 Super Constellation service from Karachi to London via Cairo, leaving at 6 p.m. on a Tuesday and arriving at London Airport at 9 a.m. the next day. In 1958, PIA bought a pair of L-1049H passenger/cargo convertible Super Connies with large freight doors; these were used for both passenger and freight services to LAP. The last PIA Super Constellation passenger schedule to London was in October 1960 but the cargo flights continued until 1966. (Jacques Guillem collection)

EL AL inaugurated services to London from Lydda (Tel Aviv) in 1950 using DC-4 4X-ACC. Its seven DC-4s were also used for transatlantic charters to New York but this route was upgraded to a scheduled service after EL AL's acquisition of five Lockheed L-049 Constellations in the early 1950s. The Connie purchase was not straightforward as two of them had fallen foul of the FBI for being illegal exports to Israel. This is 4X-AKD, seen in August 1960. (Christian Volpati collection)

➤ Brand-new EL AL Britannia Series 313 4X-AGB was displayed at the Farnborough Air Show in September 1957 prior to delivery on 19 October. One week later it flew a route-proving flight to New York followed by the inaugural NY service via LAP on 22 December. EL AL Britannia adverts boasted 'No Goose–No Gander', as the aircraft could miss out stops at Goose Bay and Gander thanks to their range. After its sale to Air Spain, it arrived on 3 March 1967 in this hybrid scheme before becoming EC-BFL and leaving on 30 April. (Daniel Tanner collection)

◄ Carrying a Bristol Proteus engine from an EL AL Britannia, Arkia's Dakota 4X-AES was seen in September 1958. The Dakota would fly on to Bristol to leave the engine there for overhaul before returning to Israel. Arkia's contract to carry these engines lasted from 1958 to 1963 and several different aircraft were used. In 1963, the EL AL Britannia fleet was reduced to just two aircraft and daily utilisation dropped from nine hours in 1958 to just four and a half, leaving Arkia with very little work, so the engine shuttle was stopped. An old Israeli Air Force Dakota is on external display at Eilat Airport painted in full Arkia colours as 4X-AES. (A.J. Aviation)

◄ Ghana Airways commenced services to LAP using leased BOAC Stratocruisers, with G-ANTZ flying the inaugural service on 15 July 1958. The country even issued a set of stamps to commemorate the event. Stratocruiser G-ANTY performed the last Stratocruiser service to LAP on 31 May 1959 just as they were being switched to using BOAC Britannias, with G-ANBL flying the first service on 14 April 1959 in full BOAC colours with Ghana titles and flag, exactly as seen on G-ANBK on 3 July 1960. (Jacques Guillem collection)

⬆ Ghana Airways was delighted with the performance of the Britannias and ordered a pair of long-range Series 309s, 9G-AAG and 9G-AAH. Alpha Golf was delivered in August 1960 and Alpha Hotel, seen here, that November. The 1961 timetable shows the Britannias flying three times a week to Accra. (Angus Squire)

➤ In 1960, Ghana started a flirtation with the Soviet Union and bought eight Ilyushin Il-18 turboprops, with a couple of these appearing at LAP in 1961–62. Here 9G-AAL is seen after arriving from Gatwick on 8 June 1961. It had brought in the President of Mali (a recent recipient of a gift of BEA Dakotas) on a state visit to see the queen. (Angus Squire)

▲ The 1961-built Ghana Airways V.838 Viscount 9G-AAU was delivered via London on 28 November that year. One of three operated on schedules connecting Accra to Lagos and Accra to Dakar via the West Coast service, all three returned to the UK when major servicing was carried out by Fields. 9G-AAU is seen here in February 1966. Note the removable 'slipper' tanks fitted to each wing that were used to extend the range either for delivery flights or for long sectors. Brooklands Museum in Surrey has a pair of these tanks on display next to the nose from RAE Vickers Viscount XT575, which carried them in service. (Chris Knott collection)

◄ Soviet aid to Nasser's independent Egypt included the supply of cheap Soviet-built airliners, including ten Antonov An-24Bs worth $2.3 million. Entering service from 1965, they were used alongside DC-6s to replace the United Arab Airlines (UAA) Viscounts on domestic services. In August 1965, UAA launched a purely domestic subsidiary airline using the Misrair title, which had originally been used between 1949 and 1958. However, Misrair only lasted ten years before it was absorbed into the parent company, having suffered from high debts and a poor safety record. An-24B SU-AOC (and sister ship SU-AOL) made two visits on cargo charters on 21 and 23 October 1967. (Author's collection)

➤ After merging the national airlines of Egypt and Syria in 1960, the Egyptian airline Misrair became UAA. In 1971 the countries split, with UAA becoming Egyptair. Freshly painted DC-6B SU-ANP, one of seven bought in the USA to replace Viscounts on domestic services, visited on 14 June 1965 on its delivery flight to Egypt. (Jacques Guillem collection)

▲ Egypt's flirtation with Soviet-built airliners in the 1960s led to the purchase of four long-range Ilyushin Il-18Ds. They were not very successful as one crashed in Kyrenia on approach to Nicosia and another crashed on approach to Aswan in Egypt. The other two managed to survive long enough to be repainted in the new Egyptair colours in 1971. Here is SU-AOX on a freight run from Cairo in October 1970. Egypt bought many of its civil and military airliner types from the Soviet Union, including Il-14s, Il-18s, Tu-154s, Il-62s, An-12s, An-24s, Il-76s and Tu-204s. (Brian Stainer)

The Iranian Airways Company, later known as Iran Air, was founded in May 1944. Scheduled services to London with Boeing 727s appear in the 1968 timetable, so the appearance of DC-6A/B EP-AEV a couple of times in 1970 was purely as a freighter. EP-AEV had been purchased from Pan American in January 1965 and it stayed with the company until 1974. The mythical bird on the fin is a Homa, the Persian bird of happiness. (Jacques Guillem collection)

Convair 440 PH-CGE was a visitor around 1959 after it was leased by KLM in January 1958 to the Iranian Oil Exploration and Producing Company N.V. It carries the name 'Heen en Weer II', which is Dutch for 'back and forth'. No, I don't know why! It also has the company titles in Arabic, Dutch and English and the registration is also in Arabic beneath PH-CGE on the fin. After the lease it was returned to KLM, which sold it in November 1963. (VIP Photoservice)

➤ With a fleet of three V.735 Viscounts delivered in late 1955, Iraqi Airways was able to start its first Viscount service, which was from Baghdad to London. On 16 April 1956, YI-ACM operated a proving flight from Baghdad, followed a month later by the inaugural service. Iraqi was still serving London with Viscounts in 1966 when this shot of YI-ACM was taken, but by 1968 it was using Tridents and the Viscounts were relegated to domestic and regional schedules. On 2 May 1958, YI-ACM was damaged in a hard landing at LAP and later patched up for a ferry flight to Marshalls of Cambridge for repairs. In August 1966, the nose leg broke off during an emergency landing at Baghdad but the old lady lived on to be sold to Alidair in 1978. (Jacques Guillem collection)

▲ Starting in June 1958, Kuwait Airways leased a variety of Viscounts, with this one, 9K-ACD, the only example to be given a Kuwaiti registration. Between February 1963 and February 1967 9K-ACD was leased from BOAC Associated Companies and is seen here complete with underwing slipper tanks after arriving on 1 November 1966. It flew to Wymeswold on the 3rd, where it was overhauled after being sold to BKS. (Brian Stainer)

◄ Now long forgotten, Central African Airways (CAA) was once an important player on the African airline scene with a large fleet based in Southern Rhodesia, Northern Rhodesia and Nyasaland for local and domestic services. CAA became an associate company with BOAC and from April 1953, CAA, BOAC and South African Airways (SAA) pooled resources and CAA Vikings were used for the four-day 'Zambezi' service to London. New Vickers Viscounts replaced the Vikings from August 1958. Ex-BEA Viking VP-YNF, seen here in the winter of 1958–59, was one of twelve Vikings operated by CAA over a twelve-year period. (J.J. Halley via Air-Britain Historians)

➤ The 1947 SAA timetable shows its Skymasters flying from Johannesburg to London via Kisumu, Khartoum and Castel Benito three times a week. SAA's London flights were upgraded from August 1950 after it received its first brand-new L-749 Constellation, which visited LAP on its delivery flight in May 1950. Seen here is ZS-BMH, which was the very last DC-4 to be built in 1947. The aircraft has survived with the South African Airways Historic Flight and in 2018 the author sampled a flight in it. (Tony Breese collection)

➤ Based in Beirut and formed as a charter operator in 1950 with help from Pan American, Lebanese International Airways (LIA) began scheduled flights in January 1956. By 1967, LIA was flying joint schedules with Middle East Airlines Air Liban (MEA) to Heathrow using Comets and VC10s. Flying stopped in January 1969 after most LIA aircraft were destroyed by an Israeli military raid on Beirut International Airport. One of those wrecked was this DC-7, OD-AEI, alongside sister ship OD-AEK and both LIA's Convair 990s. LIA was then taken over by MEA. (John Coupland via Paul Seymour)

◄ The BEA maintenance base in September 1960 held Dakota G-AJHZ in its freshly painted colours with Nigeria Airways titles. The airline had leased three Dakotas from BEA for Princess Alexandra's West African tour when she represented the queen when granting independence that October. All three departed from London on the morning of 24 September using Nigerian Airways call signs. G-AJHZ returned in March the following year and entered service with Jersey Airlines. By late 1970, G-AJHZ was derelict at Las Palmas, Gando International Airport. (Jacques Guillem collection)

◄ From 1958, BOAC associate company Nigeria Airways chartered BOAC aircraft for its London–Lagos schedule. Initially using Stratocruisers, it switched to Britannias from April 1959. Bristol Britannia 102 G-ANBA was used by Nigerian in 1959–60 carrying this slightly modified BOAC colour scheme complete with the Nigerian flag on the fin. (Martin Fenner collection)

➤ Compañia de Aviacíon Trans-Peruana began flying as an air taxi company in 1961. By 1964, non-scheduled freight services had begun with a C-82 Packet and later with Curtiss C-46 Commandos. In October 1967, Trans-Peruana joined the big boys when it bought four L-749A Constellations from Avianca to operate domestic passenger services from its base at Lima. In late 1968, the airline 'bought' this Viscount 806 G-APJU from BEA. It was painted up and parked outside the BEA maintenance area awaiting payment, which never came. Seen here on 9 February 1969, it later went to Mandala Airlines after a repaint at Prestwick. Trans-Peruana filed for bankruptcy in September 1970. (Fred Barnes)

➤ Formed in 1948 as a branch of Air France with the help of the Tunisian Government and private investors, Tunis Air began operations the following year with a small fleet of DC-3s on routes that were previously flown by Air France. Once the airline had acquired a leased DC-4 in 1954, longer routes commenced into Europe. Caravelles began to replace the well-used DC-4s from August 1961 but a couple of them did soldier on until 1969, when a Nord 262 arrived in the fleet. This is DC-4-1009 F-BILL leased from Air France in 1965 on a charter to LAP. (Tony Breese)

◄ Transporte Aereo Rioplatense (TAR) operated two Canadair CL-44s and one Yukon on worldwide cargo charters from its base at Buenos Aires. The airline's second CL-44D, LV-JZM, is seen during the airline's first visit on 17 June 1972; however, this actual aircraft had previously visited during its lease by Trans Mediterranean Airways from Slick Airways in 1967–68. Withdrawn from service at Ezeiza in 1980, it was eventually scrapped a decade later. (Author's collection)

◄ Delivered to American Airlines in 1946, this very early DC-6 was sold to Air Jordan of the Holy Lands Ltd in 1960 and was delivered to Amman via Frankfurt in September that year. JY-ACE and its sister ship JY-ACF operated domestic and international services alongside a DC-4, a Convair 240 and a DC-3 for just a year. On 29 August 1961, JY-ACF was airborne for Beirut when it was instructed to return to Amman after the airline's operating certificate was cancelled. Both DC-6s later 'escaped' to the American Airlines representative in Beirut. Air Jordan was famous for its 'Below-Sea-Level Flying Club' – look it up! This aircraft, possibly the oldest surviving DC-6, still exists at Bad Laer near Osnabrück in Germany. (Jacques Guillem collection)

▲ Trans Arabia Airways (TAA) in Kuwait bought this DC-6B G-ARTO from American Airlines on 5 October 1961. It arrived at LAP on the 11th for work by Fields prior to delivery. In November 1962, it took up the new Kuwait markings of 9K-ABA. In 1960, TAA provisionally ordered a pair of Argosy freighters but the order lapsed and it bought three DC-6Bs instead. Although the airline's timetable quoted a start date of 1 April 1963 for a service to London, due to arguments with BOAC associate company Kuwait Airways, it did not arrive until 6 July 1963. In April 1964, the Kuwaiti government bought TAA and merged it with Kuwait Airways. (Brian Stainer)

➤ Skymaster HZ-AAG was bought by Saudi Arabian Airlines from Transocean Airlines in 1952 and in early 1964 it and two other Saudi C-54s were acquired by British Eagle International Airlines so it could fulfil the IT contracts of Starways, which it had taken over. Interestingly the deal was that Saudi Arabian would take a pair of British Eagle DC-6s in exchange for the three C-54s. This is HZ-AAG after arriving at LAP on 16 February 1964 before it flew off to Prestwick, where Scottish Aviation overhauled and repainted it in full British Eagle colours as G-ASPN. (Author's collection)

▲ Having bought five new and one second-hand Series 800 Viscounts from Vickers in 1958–59 for domestic services in Brazil, Viaçâo Aerea Sao Paulo S.A. (VASP) later bought a job lot of ten V.701 Viscounts from BEA at the end of August 1962. PP-SRJ, seen here in November that year, was delivered London–Renfrew–Keflavik in February 1963, staying in service with VASP until February 1969. In the mid-1970s it ended up in a children's zoo, where it managed to survive until it was rescued and moved to Araçariguama in 2006. There it was put on poles at the Praça Santos Dumont on top of a hill. Sadly the park is now very scruffy and the Viscount equally so. (Jacques Guillem collection)

◄ The illustrated HZ-ADB was one of the pair of DC-6A/Cs exchanged for the C-54s and it flew with Saudi Arabian Airlines until it was donated to Yemen Airways in 1971. The other DC-6A/C exchanged was HZ-ADA, which survived to become G-APSA and is now preserved at the South Wales Aviation Museum. (Daniel Tanner collection)

➤ The first visit of an Ariana propliner to London was DC-3 YA-AAB, which arrived on 31 August 1957 en route to Nottingham Tollerton for overhaul by Fields. This Douglas DC-6 YA-DAN was one of two DC-6As registered in Afghanistan. Both were switched from European services, where they were regulars at Gatwick from 1966, to regional services around 1968 and both were retired in 1972 and replaced by a Boeing 727. These old ladies continued to fly until the late 1970s. (Peter Keating)

➤ The third Britannia to be purchased by Cubana is seen in May 1959 at Heathrow prior to its delivery flight to Havana. Commanded by Capt. William Cook, who was born in Preston, Cuba, to British parents, it carried a 'provisional' Cuban registration CU-P670, which was used for testing and the delivery flight. This was later changed to the permanent registration CU-T670. Cook's log book shows that it visited Heathrow to clear Customs and to pay 'Departure and Purchase Taxes' before departing for Cuba. In 1963, it was leased to ČSA and prior to its retirement in Havana in 1978 it used to return to Luton for maintenance by Monarch Engineering. (Jacques Guillem collection)

◄ Founded in Beirut in 1953 to carry fresh fruit, vegetables and meat around the Middle East on behalf of oil companies, Trans Mediterranean Airways (TMA) initially flew a pair of leased Avro Yorks. More regular flights were extended to London from spring 1959, by which time the airline was acquiring DC-4s, the first two arriving in May 1959. One of those was OD-ADK, seen here in March 1965, taking a rest on the south-side ramp next to an Egyptian Air Force Antonov An-12. (Angus Squire)

◄ Steady growth allowed TMA to buy pressurised DC-6A/Bs in 1963. The first one appeared in March 1964 and the last DC-4 to visit was in March 1970. By 1967, the fleet consisted of six DC-6A/Bs and two DC-4s, with a Pacific Western L-100-20 Hercules leased for the busy summer schedules. (Author's collection)

◄ Other prop types used by TMA at this time and seen at Heathrow included Canadair CL-44s leased from Seaboard World and Slick Airways. The airline even used this freight-configured Lockheed L-1649A Starliner (N179AV) leased from Air Venturers. It carried small TMA stickers and made a few visits between 9 October 1966 and 17 February 1967. (Pierre-Alain Petit collection)

▲ The L-100 Hercules leased for three months in 1967 by TMA from Pacific Western of Canada was CF-PWO. Delivered new to PWA in May 1967, a couple of months later it went to TMA and after its return to Canada it crashed in Peru in 1969. (Pierre-Alain Petit collection)

◄ The leap into pure jet equipment started in 1967 with a leased Boeing 707, but the propliners weren't finished yet, especially as the leased swing-tail CL-44s could carry almost twice as much as the DC-6A/B. From September 1968, TMA leased CL-44s from Gatwick-based Transglobe Airways but it sadly ran out of cash that November, leaving TMA to rely again on its DC-6s until the CL-44s returned to service the following spring. The CL-44s were returned in late 1970, leaving TMA's five DC-6s to soldier on until the last service was flown from Beirut to Stockholm in August 1973. (Pierre-Alain Petit collection)

▲ Transatlántica Argentina SA de Aeronavigación was set up by some ex-air force officers in early 1957; it initially intended to fly to Switzerland in a DC-4 but leased a pair of L-1649 Starliners instead. The first service was on 21 September 1960 from Buenos Aires to Geneva. Having completed the weekly service to Geneva, one of its (now) three Starliners (LV-GLH) arrived at London Airport three days late on 2 November 1960 while on a trip to demonstrate it to Skyways as a replacement for its Constellation freighters. It returned to Argentina on 5 November but crashed on landing at Rio on 19 June 1961. Money problems stopped the airline flying in the winter of 1961–62 and it was soon declared bankrupt, with all services transferred to Aerolineas Argentinas. (Zoggavia)

➤ Persian Air Services (PAS) was founded in 1954 as an all-cargo airline with technical support from Skyways (UK). PAS initially flew Avro Yorks until, in 1959, it leased a pair of DC-4s from SABENA for freight services to Europe. In 1960, SABENA leased PAS one of its Douglas DC-7Cs for passenger services as EP-ADU, which returned to SABENA in 1961 and was replaced by DC-7C(F) EP-AEP, seen here in the central area. By the summer of 1960, PAS was flying DC-7Cs to London twice a week. PAS merged with Iranian Airways in February 1961 to form United Iranian Airlines, which later evolved into Iran National Airlines/Iran Air. (Jacques Guillem collection)

▲ Sold by Alaska Airlines to Air Guinée in 1963, Douglas C-54D N95490 transited London on 8 July 1963 while on its delivery flight. On arrival at Conakry, it was re-registered as 3X-KRS. Air Guinée had started out with assistance from the Soviets, who supplied an Ilyushin Il-14 but in December 1962 it signed a contract with Alaska Airlines for assistance with airline management and the supply of two DC-6s. They were never delivered, but a pair of C-54s were supplied to replace an Ilyushin Il-18. The Alaska Airlines contract collapsed after six months and both aircraft were grounded after a couple of years and dumped in the grass at Conakry. (Tony Breese)

◄ This Skymaster was bought by Air Liban in June 1954 and flown on services radiating from Beirut to destinations as far as Paris until replaced by a DC-6 and a Caravelle. Air Liban entered into a marketing arrangement with MEA in 1963, with the fleets of both carriers then adopting the illustrated livery. Air Liban was later fully merged into MEA. OD-ACI is seen here near to the end of its relatively short airline career on 26 July 1963, possibly on its only visit. It arrived from Beirut, flew a return trip to Renfrew, and then returned home via Rome on the 28th. (Tony Breese collection)

➤ The first scheduled passenger service by Air India from Bombay to London using one of its three Lockheed L-749 Constellations was on 8 June 1948. Illustrated is L-1049C Super Constellation VT-DGM 'Rani of Ind', which joined the fleet in 1954. One of ten in the fleet, when it was retired it was sold along with five others to the Indian Air Force in 1962. Note the very rare Air India Morris MO vans used by the engineers in London. (Author's collection)

➤ Dakota G-AGIU in March 1961 prior to its delivery flight to Mali in West Africa. Previously operated by both BOAC and BEA, it had been sold by BEA to the Ministry of Aviation on 17 March 1961 and flown to London, where Fields prepared it for delivery. G-AGIU was one of three ex-BEA Dakotas donated by the British Government via the Ministry of Aviation to Mali at a cost of £70,000 to help it start its new airline. Transferred from the MoA on 27 March, it departed on the 31st and after arrival it was registered as TZ-ABB. Despite the free gift from the UK, the Mali Government decided to buy its next airliners from the Soviet Union and soon the airline had Il-14s, Il-18s, An-2s and Mi-2 helicopters. (J.J. Halley via Air-Britain Historians)

◄ By March 1967, Brothers Air Services (BASCO) was operating a pair of ex-BKS Dakotas on local services from Aden and in 1968–69 it bought an additional DC-3 from BUA plus four DC-6Bs. However, the enterprise did not last long after the British left Aden and the country became the People's Republic of South Yemen. Commenting on BASCO, one local British businessman reported, 'They had no idea what they were doing!' The airline was nationalised and the surviving aircraft were transferred to Alyemda, with two DC-6Bs impounded at Brussels. This is (BASCO) DC-6B 7O-ABL on 2 July 1970 while chartered to BEA. (John Coupland via Paul Seymour)

◄ Britannias were a rare sight in January 1979 when Air Faisal's Britannia G-BEMZ appeared on a freight flight. Founded in 1975 by two British Indian businessmen who wanted to bring fresh produce into their shops in Birmingham from the Persian Gulf, Air Faisal bought an ex-RAF Britannia freighter (G-BDLZ) and after some hassles with the CAA began flights using Air India call signs. G-BEMZ was the second Britannia (also ex-RAF), which was registered in February 1977. In August 1978, G-BEMZ was impounded at Manston after the discovery of 100kg of cannabis inside. The airline lost its AOC, the boss ended up in jail, and with G-BDLZ being scrapped after suffering corrosion caused by animal urine, Air Faisal was finished. (Author's collection)

➤ TSA (Transcontinental SA) took delivery of a pair of Britannias that had remained unsold since they were originally built for BOAC. Modified to 308 Series with 104 seats, LV-PPJ departed London Airport for Buenos Aires on 16 December 1959, with LV-PPL following the next day. Company advertising prematurely boasted of starting services on 19 November to New York via Sao Paolo and Rio but that was delayed. TSA did not keep up with payments to Bristol Aircraft and in October 1961 the fleet was impounded, LV-GJC (ex LV-PPL) in New York and LV-GJB (ex LV-PPJ) in Buenos Aires. Both were bought by British Eagle, with Juliet Bravo (seen here) arriving on 16 January 1964 and Juliet Charlie arriving on 23 February. LV-GJB became G-ANCF, which is currently preserved by the Britannia Aircraft Preservation Trust at Liverpool Airport. (Jacques Guillem collection)

➤ When Rhodesia was put under embargo by the UN, it retaliated by closing the border to Zambia, cutting off the supply lines for, among other things, fuel. The Zambian Government acquired two Hercules to airlift copper from N'dola to Dar-es-Salaam with fuel carried on the return. Two additional C-130s were bought and in April 1967 a fifth aircraft (9J-REZ) was purchased, which was leased to Zambian Air Cargoes with just 'Zambia' titles. Due to a fall in copper prices, losses were incurred and on 31 March 1969, Zambian Air Cargoes stopped flying. (Jacques Guillem collection)

◄ Syrian Airways started flying in 1947 with a pair of Beech 18s and three Dakotas acquired with technical support from Pan American. Four DC-4s joined the fleet in 1954–55, including this C-54A, which also flew for United Arab Airlines from 1958 to 1961 before it was transferred to Syrian Arab Airlines as YK-ADA. The London service that commenced in 1964 was switched to Caravelles the following year. In 1966 YK-ADA was damaged beyond repair in a landing accident at Damascus. (Brian Stainer)

◄ It doesn't get much rarer than this! Douglas C-74 Globemaster 1 HP-385 operated by Aeronaves de Panama performed a cargo charter from London to Egypt on behalf of United Arab Airlines and is seen here on 27 March 1963. HP-385 was one of three C-74s operated and was used to carry cattle from their base in Copenhagen to the Middle East. These cattle operations are regaled in the book *The Lord God Made Them All* by the famous vet James Herriot. Named 'Heracles', HP-385 crashed near Marseilles on 9 October 1963 after taking off at night from the wrong runway. Sister ship HP-379 became a film star when it was painted in fake Chinese markings for the film *The Italian Job*. (Author's collection)

➤ Kenya-registered East African Airways Canadair C-4 Argonaut VP-KNY. Formed by the governments of Kenya, Uganda, Zanzibar and Tanganyika, the East African Airways Corporation (EAAC) came into being in January 1946 with a small fleet of Dragon Rapides. After signing an agreement with BOAC in 1956, four BOAC Argonauts were leased for longer routes, including Nairobi to London via Entebbe, Khartoum, Benghazi and Rome. On 11 April 1962, VP-KNY crashed and burnt out at Nairobi during a training flight. The training captain feathered a working engine rather than unfeathering the feathered engine but thankfully all survived. The Argonauts were not liked by EAAC and when the fire service arrived, the captain told them to 'let it burn!' (Edward Huggett)

➤ The East African Airways Argonauts were replaced by leased Britannias from BOAC and British & Commonwealth Airlines (later BUA). Illustrated is Britannia G-ANBL taxying along to the north side in 1962; the original image reveals that the EAAC fuselage titles were removable stickers placed over the BOAC letters, so enabling BOAC to change titles without repainting. (Pete Cannon)

◄ A surprise visitor on 1 January 1978 was this Convair 240 N12WA on its delivery flight to PEI – Pan Egypt International. Arriving from Manchester as 'Papa Echo India', this 1948-built machine was re-registered in Egypt as SU-AZW and was reportedly withdrawn from use and stored at Cairo in 1982. On a visit to the Cairo ATC control tower in December 1989, the author spied it on a distant aircraft dump still with engines and props attached. (Author's collection)

▲ Merpati Nusantara Airlines (MNA) operated nine Vanguards between 1972 and 1987. It initially leased three aircraft from Templewood Aviation in 1972, two ex-Air Canada and one ex-BEA. They were flown on high-density routes with 139 seats out of Jakarta and despite only staying on the fleet for a short time, they were considered ideal, such that MNA bought three more from BA, including PK-MVF 'Tidar', which is seen departing after it had returned to the UK for an overhaul and fresh paint in June 1975. Sister ship PK-MVH flew the world's last Vanguard passenger flight in October 1987. (Author's collection)

7

BRITISH INDEPENDENTS

The incredible number of brave souls who threw their money into the airline business is reflected in the huge variety of British independent airlines. The biggest at London Airport were British Eagle, BKS, British Midland and Skyways, but right from the opening of the airport, the ramps at Heathrow were graced by independent operators from all over the UK, some of them scraping a living with just a solitary Dakota.

▲ The UK's last Constellation operator, ACE (Aviation Charter Enterprises) Freighters, also flew two Skymasters, including post-war DC-4-1009 G-APEZ seen in October 1964. It was brought to the UK by Starways in 1957 and was later leased to ACE Freighters in August 1964. Less than two years of service saw it retired to Baginton Airport in Coventry. ACE was put into liquidation in September 1966. (Author's collection)

➤ After the demise of Sagittair in 1972, Field Aircraft Services, which had maintained its three Argosies, formed a new freight airline called Air Bridge Carriers (ABC). Based at Castle Donington in the East Midlands, ABC initially flew to the Channel Islands to collect fresh fruit, flowers and vegetables. Two more Argosies were acquired as work grew and in 1974, Argosy G-APWW was sold while a Viscount 808 was bought from Overseas Aero Leasing. G-APRN, seen here in June 1975 needing a new paint job, was later given 'Jaguar Support Aircraft' titles for a tour of the Middle East. (Author's collection)

◄ A very chilly afternoon in December 1967 saw Air Ferry C-54 G-ASFY parked up after operating a night-time cargo schedule for BEA. Air Ferry was based at Manston and started operations with a pair of Vikings and a C-54 in March 1963. It eventually flew four C-54s, one of which was leased from Lloyd International after an Air Ferry C-54 had crashed. The airline also flew a pair of DC-6As and leased examples of Bristol Freighters, Viscounts and Carvairs. The airline shut down in 1968 with all services transferred to BUA. (Angus Squire)

◄ Autair started IT operations from Luton in 1961 using a fleet of three Dakotas, which the following year were joined by a pair of Vikings. Three ex-Swiss Airspeed Ambassadors were next to join up in 1963 and they were put to good use on the IT services, replacing the Vikings. Immaculate AS.57 Ambassador G-ALZV is seen here in March 1966 resting on the south side alongside one of the based Shell Ambassadors. (Author's collection)

➤ A Dart Herald was leased from Handley Page in April 1963 and after Autair had been bought out by Court Line in April 1965, three further Heralds including G-APWB, seen here in June 1969, joined the fleet. The airline obviously wasn't bothered about fleet commonality as it also bought a pair of HS748s in 1966. In April 1969, Autair transferred all its scheduled Luton services to Heathrow but they stopped after four months. Autair officially became Court Line Aviation Ltd on 1 January 1970 and in August 1974 the whole business went bankrupt, leaving 50,000 passengers stranded abroad. (Christian Volpati collection)

▲ Famous for its cross-Channel car ferry services, British Air Ferries operated a total of five ATL-98 Carvairs from its base at Southend between 1968 and 1979. This is G-ASDC 'Pont du Rhin' in October 1970 on a freight charter. It was later named 'Big Louie', then 'Plain Jane' after having all its paint removed. (Paul Huxford)

◄ When British World Airlines, the last UK operator of the Viscount, was winding down its fleet, it was appropriate that one of its Viscounts, G-APEY, took part in a special retirement celebration at Heathrow on 18 April 1996. Master of ceremonies was Raymond Baxter, and he was joined by a host of dignitaries that included many who had been involved with the Viscount, including Sir George Edwards, Sir Peter Masefield, Lord King, Ralph Robins (Rolls-Royce) and Captain Jock Bryce, who had been a Viscount test pilot. They all were treated to a final ride in G-APEY, which over the next eighteen months gave enthusiasts rides from Southend, Lydd, Hurn and other regional airports. In November 1997, G-APEY became the last operational Viscount in the UK. Still in good condition after forty years in service, it later served in Gabon, Zimbabwe, Equatorial Guinea, Swaziland and the Democratic Republic of Congo. (Adrian Balch)

➤ Messrs Barnby, Keegan and Stevens applied their names to a new airline, which became BKS Air Transport. It commenced flying in 1952 and by the following year was operating scheduled domestic services and some IT flights using Dakotas. Based initially at Southend, it later set up bases at Belfast, Dublin, London Airport, Leeds and Newcastle. In 1967 BKS became part of the British Air Services group and in 1970 the airline changed its name to Northeast Airlines, which survived until it was swallowed by the British Airways Regional Division in 1976. BKS Dakotas commenced a five-times weekly passenger service from Leeds to London on 3 October 1960. Dakota G-APPO, seen here in February 1964, opened a twice-weekly freight service between London Airport and Newcastle on 5 November 1963. (Author's collection)

➤ BKS operated four of the short-nose Series 102 Britannias. Proudly displaying its aircraft type on the fuselage is G-ANBK in the original colours in April 1965. This was the longest-serving Britannia in the fleet, lasting from 1964 until 1971. (Author's collection)

◄ Five examples of the world's most beautiful airliner, the Airspeed AS.57 Ambassador, were flown by BKS between the delivery of G-AMAD in July 1957 and the retirement of G-ALZR after a landing mishap at Gatwick in July 1969. In between that time the aircraft wore a variety of liveries, including the original one that was minimally changed from the previous owner, BEA, seen here on G-ALZT in April 1965. (Author's collection)

In the autumn of 1960, BKS ordered a fleet of five (later reduced to three) Avro 748s to replace the Dakotas. They proved to be a great money-spinner to BKS and bookings increased rapidly. Here is just one of the different colour schemes used by BKS on its forty-four-seater Avros. G-ARMX is seen in the pale-blue colours of Skyways Coach Air while leased to BKS in the mid-1960s. The Skyways logo on the nose features French and British flags alongside a coach and an airliner separated by wavy lines representing the English Channel. (John Coupland via Paul Seymour)

BKS leased a pair of former Air France Series 708 Viscounts from Maitland Drewery in the summer of 1961 to launch the airline into the turbine era. The first schedule was on 6 June 1961, when G-ARER flew London Airport to Newcastle. This is V.806 Viscount G-AOYL around 1969. (Jacques Guillem collection)

➤ Castle Donington-based British Midland Airways (BMA) was formed after Derby Airways changed its name on 1 October 1964. It had seven DC-3s for use on cargo charters and for IT services. Here freighter G-AGJV 'Millers Dale' takes a break on the south side still in its Derby Airways colours around November 1966. (Brian Stainer via Peter Marson)

➤ BMA received its first turboprop aircraft in February 1965 when its first Handley Page Dart Herald was delivered; it eventually operated a total of six. BMA initially bought three Viscounts from BUA in a deal agreed in April 1966. Operations commenced in the following January after BMA accepted delivery of the first aircraft, sixty-four-seater V.736 Viscount G-AODG, on 19 January 1967. This is V.813 Viscount G-AZLT on finals for runway 28L in September 1980. BMA would go on to operate a total of twenty-nine different Viscounts, both 700 and 800 Series, with its last one retiring in November 1988. (John Davis)

➤ Hunting Clan ordered a pair of Britannia 317s in 1957 for use on a proposed service to central Africa. This never materialised but both aircraft (G-APNA and G-APNB) were delivered wearing the colours of Hunting Clan's parent company, British & Commonwealth Shipping Company Ltd. The first service departed LAP on 31 January 1959 on a ten-day ship's crew charter. The airline won an Air Ministry contract in 1959 to carry troops from London to Hong Kong and Singapore. With 114 rearward-facing seats, the troop's accommodation was considered to be 'Unusually luxurious'. (David Howell collection)

Channel Airways Bristol 170 Freighter Mk.21 G-AIFO outside Field's hangar in May 1961. The reason for its visit may well have been for Fields to replace the fabric surfaces on the missing tail pieces. Channel Airways acquired a pair of Freighters in 1957 and used them for both passenger and freight services. The other example, G-AICT, also made a visit to Fields, probably for similar work. For years Channel proposed using them for scheduled vehicle-carrying flights and even mentioned using Blackburn Beverleys for the same purpose! The car ferry scheme was never completed but the two 'Biffos' did give good service, with the two forty-seater aircraft carrying a combined total of 46,552 passengers in 1963. (Robin Ridley collection)

Prior to BEA introducing the Argosy, they used Dan-Air London's Avro Yorks to fly freight schedules from London to Paris and to Renfrew via Manchester. Other visits by Dan-Air airliners were usually confined to weather diversions; however, this visit by DC-7BF G-ATAB may be connected to its lease to Trans Mediterranean Airlines during the summer of 1967 for freight use. Nicknamed the 'Torrey Canyon' after the oil tanker that ran aground in Cornwall in 1967 because of the oil it leaked everywhere, G-ATAB was Dan-Air's only DC-7. It was flown to Lasham for storage in 1969 and was scrapped there three years later. (John Coupland via Paul Seymour)

➤ Dan-Air's Airspeed Ambassador G-ALZO parked up on the south side next to a BKS Britannia in November 1964. G-ALZO became the last ever Ambassador to fly a scheduled service when it flew Jersey to Gatwick in September 1971. (Author's collection)

◄ Dakota G-AMSX 'Peak Dale', seen here, and G-AMSW 'Fern Dale' were bought by Derby Airways in 1959 to join four other Dakotas that until March 1959 had been operated by Derby Aviation. The Derby Airways Dakota fleet grew to eight but one was lost in a fatal accident in the Pyrenees in 1961. In July 1964, Derby Airways announced that the airline name would be changed to British Midland Airways and the Dakotas were quickly given the new titles while retaining the Derby cheatline. G-AMSX was sold in Guyana in 1966 and after ending up in Miami, it was stolen by persons unknown in 1982. (AirTeamImages)

◄ The full story behind Eagle/British Eagle/ Cunard Eagle is too complex to relate here; interested readers are recommended to check *The Eagle Years 1948–68* by David Hedges. Founded by 25-year-old Harold Bamberg in late 1947, the airline evolved to become a major player at LAP until years of battling with BOAC and the licensing authorities finally killed it off in 1968. Bamberg died in 2022, a true pioneer of British aviation. Eagle Airways amassed an impressive fleet of Vikings during the 1950s, with more than thirty being registered to the company between 1952 and 1961. Eagle bought its first Dakota in 1949 and most of the subsequent purchases were used for scheduled and charter operations, with others being converted from military configuration and sold on without flying for Eagle. This is 1945-built G-AMYB, which was bought from the RAF in 1953. (J.J. Halley via Air-Britain Historians)

◄▼ The DC-6B in full colours with Cunard Eagle titles was registered in Bermuda as VR-BBQ and leased from Canadian Pacific Air Lines in March 1961. It was re-registered G-ARWJ a year later and returned to CPAL in December 1962. The Cunard Eagle livery was applied before it was delivered but the painters messed up and painted the flying 'E' on the starboard side of the fin facing the wrong way round. The other Cunard Eagle DC-6A/C illustrated, VR-BBP, retains the colours of Overseas National, which sold it to the airline in March 1961. Its Bermudian registration was changed to G-ARMY two months later. Cunard Eagle DC-6s were regulars on the MoD service from London Airport to the Woomera Rocket Range in Australia starting in June 1962. They were replaced by Britannias from October 1963. (Christian Volpati collection, Brian Stainer via Peter Marson)

➤ Eagle and later British Eagle were famous for their busy fleet of London-based Britannias. The first Britannia service from LAP was on 6 April 1960, when military families and servicemen departed for Christmas Island in the Pacific. This is 104-seater British Eagle Britannia G-AOVB 'Endeavour' being towed by an impressive Douglas Sentinel 4x4 Heavy Aircraft Tractor in May 1968. (Martin Fenner collection)

◀ The other British Eagle aircraft illustrated is Vickers Viscount 739 G-ATDU, which was bought in Egypt in 1965 and like all of British Eagle's fleet it was given a name, in this case 'City of Liverpool'. It was scrapped in 1969. (John Coupland via Paul Seymour)

◄ Viking G-AKBH only carried Cunard Eagle's titles for a few months in early 1961 before it was sold to Airnautic in France. The Eagle empire closed down in 1968 having owned, operated, leased or traded 163 different aircraft including thirty-nine Vikings, sixteen DC-3s, seventeen Viscounts and twenty-three Britannias. Its memory lingered on at Heathrow for many years as the taxiway that passed in front of the old Eagle hangars on the east side of the airport was always known as the 'Eagle taxiway'. (Angus Squire)

► Well-travelled C-47 G-AMHJ, with just Hunting on the nose, was bought in 1951. Hunting Air Transport merged with the Clan Line shipping group in 1953 resulting in a new name – Hunting-Clan Air Transport (HCA). (AirTeam Images)

➤ HCA commenced IT services from LAP in May 1958 using a fleet of eight Vickers Vikings, whose main business was long-range trooping flights for the British MoD and colonial coach-class routes down to Africa. This is Viking 639/1 G-AHPB in August 1958. (Christian Volpati collection)

◄ HCA became the first British independent airline to order Viscounts, in 1953. Viscount 759D G-AOGG is seen here outside the company's hangar not long after it had made its first flight on 2 November 1956 from Brooklands to Wisley, where it was fitted out internally. Along with its sister ship G-AOGH, the pair were found to be surplus to requirements after HCA transferred its Newcastle routes to Dragon Airways and neither aircraft entered service. A few months later they were sold to Icelandair. (Chris Knott collection)

▲ Check out the sight of all four radials purring away on Invicta's Skymaster G-ASPM in the cargo area in 1975. This was one of a pair purchased by Invicta Airways from British Eagle in 1965. It became a freighter with Invicta Air Cargo following a failed merger with British Midland Airways early in 1969. It was sold in Africa in September 1972, where it operated in South Africa and later Zaire. (Jacques Guillem collection)

> Lloyd International was formed in 1961 by a couple of shipping partners. Brian Lloyd gave the airline its name and Alistair Macleod gave it its logo, which was from his family crest and consisted of a castle turret from Dunvegan on the Isle of Skye. They bought a pair of Britannias (G-AOVP and G-AOVS) from BOAC in 1965. G-AOVS, seen here, was leased to British Eagle for passenger services from August to November that year. Lloyd ceased operations on 16 June 1972 and G-AOVS finished its career as a film star in the 1979–80 TV series *Buccaneer* carrying 'Redair' titles. (John Coupland via Paul Seymour)

◄ Based at Leeds (Yeadon) Airport, North-South Airlines Ltd commenced ad hoc passenger and freight charters in March 1959 using a DH Heron G-ANCI, which first appeared at LAP in May that year. Further Herons were leased, followed by a pair of Bristol 170 Freighters in passenger configuration. The airline's first Dakota, G-ALXK, seen here, was bought from BEA in July 1961. Note the money-saving minimal colour scheme change from its BEA service. North-South suffered all its life from financial troubles alongside passenger complaints, so it was no surprise when in January 1962 its creditors wound up the company. (Jacques Guillem collection)

At Heathrow in 1971, Northeast Airlines had six former BEA Viscount 806s and one lone Bristol Britannia G-ANBK, seen here in July that year. It was used as a back-up to rescue the flying programme when one of the airline's 'truculent' Tridents went u/s, usually on the scheduled Heathrow–Newcastle route. One engineer told the author that the Britannia was in a very tatty condition and once, after a hard landing at Heathrow, several ceiling panels fell into the aisle along with a lot of dust and debris, exposing all the cables and pipes above. The very polite British passengers naturally apologised to each other as they brushed down their suits! (Bob Wall collection)

Northeast Airlines painted its Viscount and Trident fleet in this 'yellowbird' livery following the airline's name change on 1 November 1970. This is Viscount G-AOYH fronting a line-up of BEA Tridents in the Charlie cul-de-sac. Note the Northeast Trident lurking in the background. (Author's collection)

➤ Sagittair was based at Heathrow during the early 1970s with a fleet of Beech 18 freighters that were used initially on regular night flights to Geneva carrying newspapers. One night after take-off, flames were seen coming from an engine and with miles of runway still left, the aircraft landed straight ahead and cleared the runway. The pilot got out and, according to the staff in the VCR, he beat out the flames with what appeared to be his hat. He took off again, only for the same thing to happen! During a postal strike in 1971, Sagittair was the only British operator specifically licensed by the ATLB and the GPO to carry mail to Europe. That year also saw the arrival of the first of Sagittair's three AW 650 Argosy freighters but debts had built up and the company collapsed in September 1972. (Author's collection)

▲ The Shell Petroleum company has an aviation section that can be traced right back to 1927, when it took delivery of a brand-new Cirrus Moth. Shell's aviation fleet expanded all across the world and after using bases at Croydon and Blackbushe, its UK base was moved to LAP south side in 1960. Shell executives departing for business meetings could use a variety of propliner types including a pair of Airspeed Ambassadors (this is G-AMAG) in addition to DH Herons and a Grumman Gulfstream 1. Shell Aircraft Ltd became Shell Aircraft International in 2000 and is currently based at Rotterdam, with some seriously expensive business jets in its fleet. (Chris Knott collection)

After twelve years serving BEA, Vanguard G-APEI was earmarked for lease to Silver City Airways (the second iteration of this airline) and was given a quick paint job at Heathrow, where it is seen in October 1973. Silver City was already operating Vanguard G-AYLD and needed another to help with freight contracts; however, the deal fell through and after sitting outside for several weeks, G-APEI was dragged back inside and given full BEA colours. It then returned to service alongside three other passenger Vanguards. (Christian Volpati collection)

Skyways was a major British charter airline with a large fleet of propliners that started in 1946 with a pair of Lancastrians, a pair of Yorks, a Rapide and a Dove. The first commercial flight was from London to Basra in a York for the Anglo-Iranian Oil Co. in May 1946. Here is York G-AGNV at rest in the early 1960s. (Author's collection)

➤ Four BOAC L-749A Constellations were acquired by Skyways in 1959 to operate freight schedules to the Far East from London. This is G-ANUR taxying with its door open in 1962; the impressive selection of aircraft in the background include Percival Prince G-AMLZ, which was maintained by British Eagle. The Connie was transferred to Euravia later that year. (Author's collection)

◄ Lympne-based Skyways Coach-Air bought three new Avro 748s in 1962–63 and they initially served on the airline's famous coach-air schedules between London and Paris flying the airborne section of the route between Lympne and Beauvais. The illustrated G-ARMX was leased to British Eagle in 1965 to fly the London–Liverpool schedule. After the airline collapsed in January 1971, G-ARMX flew with Dan-Air and Air BVI before it was donated to the Manchester Airport Fire Service. (Robin Ridley collection)

▲ Exeter-based South West Aviation Ltd (SWA) was formed in August 1966 and commenced air taxi operations with a Piper Aztec. In early 1968, the airline leased Astazou-powered Skyvan Series 2 G-ATPF from Short Brothers for freight charters from Exeter and Bristol and this appeared at Heathrow that May. In July it acquired a C-47B Dakota in the shape of G-APBC, seen here looking very smart in its modified British Midland colours in March 1970. (Jacques Guillem collection)

➤ In July 1968, SWA leased Series 3 Skyvan G-AWCS to replace the Series 2, which was returned to Shorts. In July 1971, fourteen-seater G-AWCS commenced daily passenger services from Plymouth to Heathrow and when it was returned to Shorts for overhaul in November 1971 it was replaced by a Humber Airways BN-2 Islander. The Plymouth schedule stopped in January 1972 and later that year SWA was bought out by Air Freight. (Author's collection)

➤ Initially set up at Blackpool in the late 1940s, Starways Ltd soon moved to Liverpool and received its first large airliner in the shape of a Dakota in 1950. The airline moved from charters to IT operations and acquired more Dakotas in 1952. The airline's first schedule to LAP was in 1955 using Dakotas from Liverpool. In 1957 Starways received its first DC-4, G-APEZ, seen here in 1962, and later operated seven Skymasters in total. (Tony Clarke collection)

➤ After Starways acquired its first turboprop airliner, an ex-Air France Viscount 708 in 1961, it flew their Liverpool–London schedule starting on 12 June. Starways tried hard to get licences for other routes but most were denied by the UK authorities and the airline collapsed and was taken over by British Eagle at the end of 1963. G-AMOE was a British Eagle Viscount 701 given Starways titles as their routes were still held in the Starways name. (Ron Roberts via Barry Friend)

◄ Having started operations with a fleet of Vikings in 1958, Southend-based Tradair Ltd bought a pair of Aer Lingus Viscount 707s in 1960. These made several visits to LAP flying under sub-contract for major airlines that had fleet shortages. Here is G-APZB on 6 August 1960. Financial problems grounded the Viscounts in 1961–62, leaving all remaining services to be flown by Vikings. (Jacques Guillem collection)

➤ Originally formed to operate long-range ad hoc cargo charters using a pair of DC-4s in 1962, Trans Meridian later obtained a DC-7CF in 1964 and another in 1966, with the airline eventually using five different DC-7CFs but with only a maximum of three in service at one time. A wise upgrade to the fleet occurred after Flying Tigers started to sell off its swing-tail Canadair CL-44s. Trans Meridian bought a pair and they arrived at Stansted in 1969. This is DC-7CF G-ATMF, which was bought by Trans World Leasing in 1966 and immediately sub-leased to Trans Meridian as 'Sir Benjamin'. (Jacques Guillem collection)

➤ From early in 1964, British Westpoint flew passenger services from London to Lille on behalf of Air France. Dakotas G-AMDB and G-ALYF received additional 'Air France' stickers on the fuselage. In total, Westpoint, which was based at Exeter Airport, operated five Dakotas. In September 1965, the airline was bought out by Metropolitan Air Movements but Westpoint continued to fly under its own name until May 1966, when it ceased operations. (Adrian Balch collection)

◄ World Wide Aviation Ltd was based at Gatwick and commenced ad hoc charters in December 1960 with this single Skymaster G-APCW leased from Trans-World Leasing Ltd. G-APCW flew a series of scheduled flights from London Airport to Reykjavík on behalf of Loftleidir before it was wet-leased to SABENA for a year from January 1961. SABENA sent it to Leopoldville in the Belgian Congo, where it flew UN relief missions. WWA suffered from cash-flow problems and eventually stopped all flying in October 1961. (Tony Breese)

BIBLIOGRAPHY

Gradidge, J.M., *The Convairliners Story*, Air-Britain Publications, 1997.

Hedges, David, *The Eagle Years 1948–1968*, The Aviation Hobby Shop.

Henderson, Scott, *The Pictorial History of BOAC and Associated Airlines*, SCOVAL Publishing, 2015.

Hengi, B.I., *Airlines Remembered: Over 200 Airlines of the Past, Described and Illustrated in Colour*, Midland Publishing, 1999.

Hillman, Peter; Jessup, Stuart; Morgan, Adrian; Morris, Tony; Ottenhof, Guus; Roch, Michael, *More Than Half a Century of Soviet Transports*, The Aviation Hobby Shop, 2004.

Littlefield, David, *A History of the Bristol Britannia*, Halsgrove Press, 1992.

Lo Bao, Phil, *An Illustrated History of British European Airways*, Browcom Group Plc, 1989.

May, Garry, *The Challenge of BEA*, Wolfe, 1971.

Merton Jones, A.C., *British Independent Airlines 1946–1976*, The Aviation Hobby Shop, 2000.

Piercey, Stephen, and later Merton Jones, Tony, *Propliner Aviation Magazine*, 1979 onwards.

Piket, Brian and Bish, Peter, *Heathrow ATC – The First 50 Years*, Zebedee Balloons Service, 2005.

Porter, Malcolm, *CL-44 Swingtail – The CL-44 Story*, Air-Britain Historians, 2004.

Powers, David G., *Lockheed 188 Electra*, World Transport Press, 1999.

Roach, J., and Eastwood, A.B., *Turboprop Airliner Production List; Piston Engine Airliner Production List*, A.J. Aviation, various dates.

Shives, Bob, and Thompson, Bill, *Airlines of North America*, Crest Line, 1984.

Simons, Graham M., *The Spirit of Dan-Air*, GMS Enterprises, 1993.

Thaxter, David, *The History of British Caledonian Airways 1928–1988*, David Thaxter, 2009.

Veronico, Nicholas, *Boeing 377 Stratocruiser*, Speciality Press, 2001.

Vomhof, Klaus, *Leisure Airlines of Europe*, SCOVAL Publishing, 2001.